The Mindful Breathing Workbook For Teens

Simple Practices To Help You Manage Stress & Feel Better Now

Matthew D. Dewar, EdD

16pt

Copyright Page from the Original Book

Publisher's Note

This publication is designed to provide accurate and authoritative information in regard to the subject matter covered. It is sold with the understanding that the publisher is not engaged in rendering psychological, financial, legal, or other professional services. If expert assistance or counseling is needed, the services of a competent professional should be sought.

INSTANT HELP, the Clock Logo, and NEW HARBINGER are trademarks of New Harbinger Publications, Inc.

Distributed in Canada by Raincoast Books

Instant Help Books
An imprint of New Harbinger Publications, Inc.
5674 Shattuck Avenue
Oakland, CA 94609
www.newharbinger.com

Cover design by Amy Shoup; Acquired by Jess O'Brien;
Edited by Rona Bernstein; Illustrations by Tara Brunner

Library of Congress Cataloging-in-Publication Data

Names: Dewar, Matthew D., author.
Title: The mindful breathing workbook for teens : simple practices to help you manage stress and feel better now / Matthew D. Dewar, EdD.
Description: Oakland : New Harbinger Publications, 2021. | Includes bibliographical references.
Subjects: LCSH: Stress in adolescence--Juvenile literature. | Meditation--Therapeutic use--Juvenile literature. | Stress management--Juvenile literature.
Classification: LCC BF724.3.S86 D49 2021 | DDC 155.5/182--dc23
LC record available at https://lccn.loc.gov/2021001047

TABLE OF CONTENTS

"Matt Dewar's book is remarkable. To take a topic that has already been written about by so many, like mindful breathing, yet do it in such a unique way that offers much new insight and practical application is outstanding! There is even a brilliant section on finding one's core life principles. This book is going to help a lot of teens better manage their emotions, focus, and energy."

—**Todd Corbin, CPC,** international speaker, certified parenting coach, and coauthor of the best-selling *Mindfulness for Student Athletes*

"A practical guide to mindfully balance your breath, body, emotions, and stress."

—**Christopher Willard, PsyD,** author of *Growing Up Mindful* and *Mindfulness for Teen Anxiety,* and faculty at Harvard Medical School

"There is no doubt that we are living in unprecedentedly stressful times. Teens are especially vulnerable to the emotional, cognitive, and physical impacts of stressors. Dewar's book is an incredibly valuable gift to teens, therapists, and parents. Teaching the importance of breath to teens can be a challenge, and Dewar demystifies this process in a way that is relatable and deeply insightful. This essential resource has been long overdue!"

—**Goali Saedi Bocci, PhD,** licensed clinical psychologist, author of *The Social Media Workbook for Teens,* coauthor of *The*

Positivity Workbook for Teens, and adjunct professor in the Pepperdine Graduate School of Education and Psychology

"While the teen years can be challenging, they are foundational—and what can be more foundational than the breath? Merging the gifts of this workbook with reflection and action, this guide serves as a 'life coach' of support for teens and the adults who love them. Full of tools and wise guidance, this workbook can launch teens into young adulthood with skills that will last a lifetime."

—**Tovi C. Scruggs-Hussein,** Tici'ess, Inc. leader and healer; creator of the EI2: Emotionally Intelligent Equity and Inclusion approach; and visionary of Racial Healing Allies™

"Along with learning emotional regulation and stress management strategies based on the science of stress, mindfulness, and breathing, Matthew Dewar offers a truly unique process for increasing the joy in your life, honoring the gift of each day, and becoming your own person. As a beloved high school teacher and wellbeing coordinator, he 'gets' teens and uses brilliant anecdotes to help make the transformative concepts in his book stick."

—**Tracy Heilers,** founder and executive director of the Coalition of Schools Educating Mindfully (COSEM), and coauthor of *Educating Mindfully*

"Matthew Dewar has written the ultimate breathing workbook for teens, and every teen should have a copy. This practical and useful guide will set the stage early for a lifetime skill of breath awareness and regulation. It is just the antidote stressed-out teens need. It's the perfect prescription for today's frazzled teens."

—**Barbara Larrivee, EdD,** author of *A Daily Dose of Mindful Moments* and *Cultivating Teacher Renewal*

"A powerful combination of practical wisdom, precise instruction, and passionate advocacy for the power of mindful breathing. Matthew Dewar has written a much-needed book that will support countless teens, and I'll be recommending it often."

—**David Treleaven, PhD,** author of *Trauma-Sensitive Mindfulness*

In memory of my dear friend and mentor, "Dr. Bill" Levin, whose love and laughter saved an anxious seven-year-old boy.

foreword

I started practicing mindfulness in my late teens, eons ago ;), but I despised mindful breathing because no one taught me why or how to do it. The only experiences I could refer to were when I went to see doctors. When I was sick, doctors wanted to hear my breathing so they put a stethoscope on my back and chest. They would tell me to "Breathe deep, long, and hard." As I did, I quickly felt short of breath, even faint, because I was breathing differently than I usually did. So when I began practicing mindfulness and my teachers asked me to focus on my breath, I thought I should breathe like I did for doctors using a stethoscope. I feared the shortness of breath and the possibility that I could faint. I almost revolted against mindful breathing.

This experience is far from what author Matthew Dewar, known as "Mr. D," calls *mindful breathing*. Turns out my fears were based on a belief about how to do it that was wrong! I have now learned just how amazing and wondrous our breath is. We just need to be taught the how-to of mindful breathing. That is what this entire book is about.

Mr. D provides a gently unfolding, step-by-step journey to turn toward and befriend your breath. We are already breathing, so why not use it to our benefit? There are vast benefits from mindful breathing. Here are a few: your mindful breaths can reduce stress, anchor you so you're grounded in the moment, be a constant resource because breathing is always with you, and provide you with information about how you're doing—physically and mentally—in every moment. By reading and working through these easy-to-understand activities throughout the four sections of this book, you too can benefit.

This book provides concrete ways to learn all about turning toward your breath and using it as a resource in your life, moment by moment. Kudos to Mr. D! He not only provides you with science, information, and education about the body's breathing and its benefits, he also supports your learning by sharing stories of his personal and professional experiences.

Imagine your breath as the hub, the information center, that can tell you about your body, thoughts, emotions, and stress level. It's also a control center that, with some skills, can improve weakened areas of your life and bolster important self-care efforts. Your breath can support all aspects of your day-to-day experience. As you start this journey of learning about your breath and the many ways to use it, remember that every moment is a new opportunity to turn toward your breath and check in with yourself. Let this awareness guide you. You can always make adjustments because every moment is a new chance to start over, to do something different to support your health and well-being.

—Gina M. Biegel, MA, LMFT

Psychotherapist, researcher, and author of many books for teens

dear reader: we're not perfect, so let's not stress about it

Writing a book like this might give the impression that the author—yours truly—has everything figured out. So, let's get something straight right away: *I don't have everything figured out.* Far from it. I've made many mistakes. I've contradicted myself countless times. I've been ungrateful and entitled. I've been mindless, even reckless. I've stressed myself out for no reason and worked myself up into fits of anxiety. No, *I'm not perfect.*

Just in case I haven't convinced you, let me share a quick little story: I dropped out of college my sophomore year without telling my parents and went to the other side of the world to live in a Zen Buddhist monastery, where I got busted for sneaking out in the middle of the night for pizza. Repeatedly.

Twenty years later, I still remember the first thing I wrote in my journal after a few days at the Buddhist monastery: "I traveled almost 7,000 miles, but my mind didn't move." This came as a shock and disappointment to me because I'd hoped that my journey to the other side of the world would "move" my mind into a better place and free me from all the stress and anxiety I felt at the time. I didn't know who I was or what I wanted my life to be, so I latched onto the idea that if I went somewhere else, somewhere more beautiful and serene, somewhere with no problems, somewhere “perfect,” I could escape my worries and solve all of my problems. But here’s what actually happened: I became more conflicted and miserable there than I was at home. And so I learned one of the great lessons of life the hard way...

You can’t run from yourself.

The world is a big place, but it’s not big enough to escape from yourself—because wherever you go, there you are. You can’t outrun what you feel inside. But sometimes it takes a failed outward journey for you to begin a successful inward journey—the journey to become your own person.

We all have our own process, our own journey to work through. You have your own fears, regrets, and hopes, and I’ve got mine. But when you realize that we’re all on our own journey, you don’t feel so ashamed for being imperfect anymore. There’s no need for the constant comparisons and judgments; they only lead to self-dissatisfaction—and unnecessary stress and anxiety. The more you search for others’ approval, the more you’ll compare yourself to them, and no matter how hard you try, someone will always be more attractive, more popular, more entertaining, and more interesting than you. And the more you live by these superficial comparisons, the more critical you'll become of yourself. So, be compassionate with yourself, and with others, too. Like you, they don't want to be victims of constant comparison and judgment.

I'm not a finished product, and I never will be—nor will you. And once we accept this about ourselves, we can shift our focus from trying to "fix" our imperfections and problems—which is terribly stressful and exhausting—and begin to use them as opportunities to learn more about ourselves and what's possible for our lives. I want to make this really clear: this workbook isn't about "fixing" yourself—because you're not broken. Instead, think of this workbook as an opportunity to learn a new skill, mindful breathing, that can help you live a calmer, less anxious life.

As a high school teacher and well-being coordinator, one of the most common themes that has emerged in my work with young adults is that of the forgotten inner self. The *inner self* is the you that is most yourself because only you can access it and *feel* it. Only you can experience and know what it's like to be yourself from the inside-out—while everyone else only experiences and knows you from the outside-in. The problem is that we live in a world where, more and more, we're taught to invest too much of our time, energy, and attention in building up the "outer self." And this only leads to unnecessary stress and anxiety.

Much of stress and anxiety is rooted in a neglect of the inner self, and this is where a mindful breathing practice comes into the picture. When you learn to pay mindful attention to your breathing, you learn to pay mindful attention to your inner life. So, think of the practice of mindful breathing as an invitation from your inner self to stop chasing perfection and come back home. Perfection might not be attainable, but a life of less stress, more calm, and deeper well-being is attainable. All it takes is a willingness to slow down, pay attention, and *breathe*. And that's what this workbook is all about.

Let's get breathing!

a note to caring adults

"Coregulation" has become a buzzword in education and mental health. It refers to how your self-awareness and self-care skills synchronize with the emotional habits of the children and young adults you care for and oversee. The implications of this are significant: you teach and parent more with *who* and *how* you are than with the content of what you say. Emotions are much, much older than words, and whether we like it or not, our young adults' inner lives set sail to our own emotional ebbs and flows.

What this means is that we must do our own self-awareness and self-care work alongside our young adults. When they see us doing this work, they become aware of the possibility that the work can be done, that a healthy and stable emotional life is possible with practice. Just as importantly, they become aware, through your choice to personally value and prioritize self-care, that it's significant and worth the commitment. I can't think of anything more instructive than demonstrating to young adults the capacity to struggle, adapt, and evolve toward greater emotional intelligence and freedom.

So, to help your teen get the most out of this workbook, read it along with (or separately from) them, practice the skills together, and do your best to model the qualities you want to see in your teen. And have some fun! Who knows, you might even learn a thing or two!

before you begin

Mindfulness has come to mean many things to many people. A simple search on Amazon yields over 30,000 results. From books and clothing to tea and bracelets, mindfulness, in all its forms, has come to represent the definitive solution to all of our twenty-first century problems. Consequently, I think it's important to place a disclaimer up front: despite the hype, mindfulness will not cure or solve all of life's problems.

Instead of thinking of mindfulness as a solution to all problems, I offer an alternative perspective: mindfulness practice invites you to experience your life not as a problem to be solved but as an opportunity to develop greater emotional skill and well-being.

Most importantly, the word "mindfulness" comes from a Sanskrit word that means "to remember." Implicit in this notion of remembering is that we forget. The question, then, is what do we forget? That life unfolds only in the present moment. No matter how far away you think you've drifted from yourself, you can "remember" your way home by following your breath back to the present moment, back to yourself. This idea of remembering to come home to ourselves in the present moment and using our breathing as the pathway there is ultimately how mindfulness is presented and practiced throughout this workbook.

Meet Mindful Breathing

Simply stated, this workbook is about mindful awareness, dealing with stress, and learning how to breathe. Now, the idea that you need to learn how to breathe might initially seem pretty absurd. I mean, after all, you've presumably been breathing fine your whole life because, well, here you are. It's understandable to assume that you know what you're doing, but I hope to show you in the course of this workbook that there's a vast difference between "normal" breathing and what I call *mindful breathing*.

The main reason you might think that breathing is just breathing is because it's an autonomic, or unconscious, process—which means that you breathe without having to think about it—and that's definitely a good thing. I'm guessing you wouldn't want to consciously breathe the 20,000 to 30,000 breaths you'll take today—or the roughly 600 million breaths you'll take over the course of your life. That would be pretty cumbersome and exhausting. The good news is that your brainstem, the oldest part of your brain (hundreds of millions of years old), says, "Hey, you, no need to worry. I got this." And lucky for you, you get to breathe without thinking so that you can pay attention to all those other awesome things that human brains get to do, like ponder the meaning of life or your pre-calc homework or what you're going to post next on social media (wink, wink). And so long story short, for the untrained breather, most breathing occurs outside of conscious awareness—with one exception: when you lose control over it.

It's likely that you only notice your breathing when it becomes irregular and loses its normal pattern. This typically happens when you're under physical or emotional stress (your physiology makes no distinction between physical and emotional stress, BTW). Maybe you've gone for a run and pushed it a little too hard and then have had to "catch your breath." Or maybe something happened that made you so upset that you got emotional and "choked up." Whatever the case might be, you rarely notice your breathing unless it's all out of sorts.

So why am I rambling on and on about your breathing? Well, because ... pay close attention here ... your breathing is the best kept secret for reconnecting with your inner self and managing your stress.

Your Breathing Tells You a Lot About Yourself

At every moment of every day, how you breathe is a window into your inner self. As sages have long said, "The breath is the mind made visible." This is because the areas of the brain that control breathing rate and emotional alertness directly influence each other.[1] This means that every emotional state—high or low—causes you to breathe in a particular way. When you're connected to yourself and calm, you breathe lightly, slowly, and deeply. When you're disconnected from yourself and anxious, you breathe heavily, rapidly, and shallowly. How you breathe is a status report on your emotional stress level at any given moment.

In your car, the dashboard has a tachometer that measures the RPMs (revolutions per minute) of your engine and tells you how hard your engine is working. It has various warning lights to communicate engine distress so that you can address any problems before the whole engine goes up in smoke. In a similar manner, your breathing is like the tachometer that measures your stress levels (i.e., your emotional RPMs) and communicates vital information about them. But your breathing also does more than gauge your stress levels: once you're aware, through your breathing, of changes to your emotional RPMs, you can then use your breathing like a gear shift to transition out of stress and into balance and calm.

Your Breathing Can Lower Your Stress Level

One of the unique things about being a human is that you can intentionally change your breathing in order to change and manage your emotional state. In this workbook, we'll focus specifically on using your breathing as a tool to decrease and control stress—though I want to make it clear that your breathing can be used to increase alertness and energy, too, but that's a matter for a different time and place (usually for activities that require high levels of energy, like athletic performance).

The more control you have over your breathing, the more control you have over your stress levels. It's that simple. No money needed. No nasty side effects. And nothing extra to add to your life—just a willingness to practice what you already have to do 20,000 to 30,000 times today. And tomorrow. And the day after that. And even though there are many other activities—like exercise, diet, and social connection, to name a few—that can help you manage your stress, only breathing is always immediately and universally accessible to everyone. Whoever you are, wherever you are, and whatever you're feeling, your breath is always right there, showing your stress levels in real time and inviting you to take the wheel of your life and downshift into a calmer state.

There's evidence that human beings have been systematically practicing breathing techniques to manage stress for at least 5,000 years.[2] Like shooting a basketball, playing the piano, carving wood, or juggling fire torches (which I really don't recommend as a stress-management technique), mindful breathing is a skill that can be developed through conscious practice. And the more you practice it, the better you get, and the better you get, the more control you develop over how you feel and how you respond to stressful internal and external circumstances. If you can mindfully breathe, you can mindfully choose how you respond to stress (instead of merely reacting to it). When you get stressed, remember this mantra: *If I can breathe, I can choose*.

In summary, your stress levels and your breathing influence each other. By increasing awareness of your breathing, you increase your awareness of your stress levels in any given moment. When you notice that your breathing and your emotions are about to redline, you can modify your breathing to downshift what you're feeling. I know from my own mindful breathing practice that the more aware I become of my breathing, the earlier I can identify and shift out of rising stress levels before they become full-blown "check engine" stress meltdowns. And this can be life changing for sure.

How to Get the Most from This Workbook

It's important to remind you that *how* you use this workbook will determine what you get out of it. Therefore, I suggest that you establish a special time and place (like before bed or first thing in the morning) that allows you to be fully present to these activities. Think of doing the activities in this book as a part of your emerging self-care practice. If you feel rushed or scattered, take a few moments to slow down and center yourself before starting the activities. There's no rush and there's no medal or prize for the reader who completes this workbook the fastest. In fact, mindful breathing is kind of like a bike race where the winner is the one who can pedal the slowest without falling off. So pedal slowly.

Last thing: this workbook is designed to be experienced from beginning to end. This means that completing the activities sequentially will most positively benefit your mindful breathing practice. If you arrive at an activity that doesn't resonate with you, do your best to be patient and try to work through it. If, after trying it, the activity continues to feel forced, then you can move on, but I encourage you to circle back to it at a later time. Once you've completed the workbook in its entirety, you'll have a better idea of which activities you'll continue to practice and which you'll put on the shelf for a later time. So let's get started!

1

SECTION ONE

Master the Basics of Mindful Breathing

Your attention is your window into the world. If you spend most of your precious time paying attention to things that make you stressed out and unhappy, then you're going to be a stressed out and unhappy person. But if you spend most of your precious time paying attention to things that make you happy and well, then you're going to be a happy and well person. So, the first step toward mastering a mindful breathing practice is unpacking the importance of attention.

1

cultivate mindful attention

Your attention is vital to your emotional well-being because what you pay attention to and how you pay attention to it are the basis of everything you experience in life. For example, imagine two people whose lives are identical. The only difference between them is what they habitually pay attention to. The first person spends all day staring at images of people on social media who they think are smarter, are better looking, and have way cooler lives. Consequently, this person is constantly reminded of the fact that they're not as good as everyone else. The second person, however, spends less time on social media and more time deliberately paying attention to all the things they're grateful for—like the fact that they're alive and have air to breathe, water to drink, food to eat, clothing to wear, a roof to shelter them, people to connect with, ideas to inspire them, goals to motivate them, and, most importantly, the opportunity to positively impact someone else's life. Consequently, they live with a deep sense of gratitude.

Now, based on these short descriptions, which person do you think experiences more stress? Which person do you think experiences more happiness and emotional wellbeing? Explain why.

____

____

____

____

My students tell me that the first person has more stress in their life because they're likely preoccupied with everything they're *not* and everything that their life *isn't.* Consequently, they're stressed out because life is a constant battle to attain the happiness they think they lack within themselves—which leads, according to my students, to a vicious cycle of stress, insecurity, anxiety, and even despair.

On the other hand, the second person, my students tell me, experiences more happiness and emotional well-being because instead of looking at everything that they lack, they pay attention to everything they already have and are filled with appreciation, contentment, and happiness.

Now the real question is ... which person sounds more like you? Are you like the first person? Or are you more like the second person? Why do you think this is the case? For example, most of the time, I'm more like the second person because I take time each day to consciously acknowledge the many ways I'm fortunate. However, this doesn't mean that I don't have days when I get lost in distraction and comparison, but I do my best to not let those days become the norm.

____

____

____

____

Well done. It's important to start by simply recognizing the power attention has on your stress levels and emotional well-being. The next step is to cultivate a special kind of attention that you need to prevent unnecessary stress and live your best life. This special kind of attention is called *mindful attention.*

The ability to cultivate mindful attention is essential for your emotional well-being. Mindful attention is attention that is *selective, focused,* and *nonjudgmental.* Let's look at these three features of mindful attention because they will launch your mindful breathing practice, ease your stress, and support your emotional well-being.

Selective Attention

Selective attention relates to *what* you choose to pay attention to. There are many things you could pay attention to, but not all of them are worth your conscious attention because not all of them are relevant to your goals. With so many websites to browse and with so much social media content to consume, it's getting more difficult to not lose ourselves—and our attention—in all the background noise. Since you're unlikely to have fewer distractions any time soon, it's up to you to protect your emotional well-being by becoming more selective about what you pay attention to.

Two things you can do to develop selective attention are to establish meaningful goals and to pay attention to what you pay attention to. Let's learn how.

Establish meaningful goals. Goals focus your attention and help you select in advance what's worth paying attention to and what's not. For example, if your goal is to have a certain GPA, then you need to organize your life around paying attention in class, taking good notes, studying, and doing homework. And when you're doing homework, you need to be paying attention to your homework, and not paying attention to anything else (like your phone!). Get the idea?

So, what are *your* goals? I know that the mere utterance of the word "goal" might send chills down your spine. At the beginning of the year, when I ask my students to create goals, they let out an audible sigh of disgust. Goals have received a bad rap, probably because too many teachers and coaches force goals on young adults without ever explaining why they are so important for managing your attention, off-setting stress, and enhancing emotional well-being.

So, in brief, here is my plug for *why* you should set goals: Goals help you become more selective with your attention because they allow you to establish in advance what is important and worth paying attention to—and, consequently, what you should ignore. Without the ability to be selective with your attention, you will continually find yourself distracted, stressed, and unhappy. Since we all want to be happy (have you ever met a person who didn't want to be happy?), it's imperative that you set goals that actually mean something to you so you can be more selective with your attention and focus on the things that will make your life better.

So, here we go ... Imagine the person you want to be in one year. Think about, and write down, your goals in the following areas:

Goal #1: In one year, my future self will look...

____

____

____

____

____

Goal #2: In one year, my future self will feel...

____

____

____

____

____

Goal #3: In one year, my future self will be able to...

Goal #4: In one year, my future self will think...

Goal #5: In one year, my future self will experience...

Nice work. You should feel good about what you've just done. Clearly defined goals help you focus on what's important and resist the distractions that cause unnecessary stress and weaken your well-being.

Now identify one thing (and it can be small) that you need to do to move closer to each goal. For example, if your goal is for your future self to feel calmer, an action toward that goal might be to practice five minutes of mindful breathing.

Action toward goal #1:

____

____

Action toward goal #2:

____

____

Action toward goal #3:

____

____

Action toward goal #4:

____

____

Action toward goal #5:

____

____

Just by creating a vision of how you want your life to unfold and by identifying what you need to do each day to get there, you're organizing your attention so it doesn't get lost in the wilderness of distraction. Now, here's the second way to develop selective attention.

Pay attention to what you pay attention to. If you're not aware of the fact that you're distracted, then you're likely going to keep wasting your attention on random, in-the-moment "stuff." What are some examples from your daily life where you allow your attention to be hijacked by distractions? In other words, what are your biggest attention-sucking distractions? Rank them in order with the approximate amount of time per day you spend on them.

Distraction	Amount of Time
1.	
2.	
3.	
4.	
5.	

Identify a distraction from this list that you'd like to minimize:

____

Why should you pay less attention to this distraction? How does it prevent you from paying attention to your goals and negatively impact your emotional well-being?

____

____

____

____

What's something related to your goals that is not on your list that you'd like to pay *more* attention to?

____

Why should you pay more attention to it? How will it positively impact your emotional well-being?

____

____

____

____

Well done. With established goals and a clear sense of what distracts you from achieving them, you'll be more selective about what you pay attention to—which will reduce stress and anxiety and help you feel better about yourself and your life. Now, on to the next aspect of mindful attention: focused attention.

Focused Attention

Focused attention relates to *how* you pay attention. It involves paying attention to one thing for a sustained period of time. Without a conscious practice to develop your focus, your brain will instinctively pay attention to whatever pops up in the moment.

For example, let's say you have to solve sixty algebra problems in a fifty-minute class period. Your ability to successfully do this requires that you pay *sustained* attention to only those sixty problems and block everything else out. During that class period you can't indulge in thinking about all the things you want to do this weekend, what you're going to wear tomorrow, or whether your best friend was kidding or not when they made fun of your shirt. All of these mental wanderings are temporarily on hold when focused attention takes the wheel of your mind.

Can you think of the last time you spent an hour paying attention to a single task without checking your phone, email, social media, or something on the internet? When was it? And what were you doing?

____

____

____

____

Describe how you felt while doing it.

____

____

____

____

Up until this point, while reading this workbook, has your attention wandered? Have you been dividing your attention among multiple tasks? If so, what other tasks? What compelled you to pay attention to these tasks?

Have you checked your phone since you started reading? How many times? What were you checking? Was it essential to check it?

Do a little experiment: Pick an activity that requires focus (like reading, doing homework, watching a movie, or talking with a friend). Do this activity and nothing else for one hour. As you perform this activity, pay attention to your attention. Notice the impulse arise to pay attention to other things and how that impulse actually feels. *But don't act on it.* Continue to focus on the activity you've dedicated the hour to. When the hour is over, pat yourself on the back and treat yourself to a small reward (assuming you actually made it the whole hour without starting another task!). Describe what this experience was like, paying particular attention to how the impulse to pay attention to something else actually felt. For example, what made it most difficult to stay focused on the activity? And how did you refocus your attention on the activity when it drifted off?

In what situation is it easiest for you to pay attention? Why do you think that is? For example, I find it easiest to pay attention when I'm reading on my front porch in the evening. I think it's easiest because I leave my phone inside. This allows me to settle into whatever I'm reading without my attention being pulled to my phone. What about you?

In what situation is it most difficult for you to pay attention? Why do you think that is? For example, students often say that it's hardest to pay attention when doing schoolwork because their phones give them immediate and endless access to other things, like the internet, music, and social media, that are much more interesting than the Pythagorean theorem or reading Billy Shakespeare!

In what situation does your ability to pay focused attention most positively impact your emotional well-being? For example, many of my students share that when they take time to be still and quiet or go for a walk outside, they feel more present to themselves and their lives because in these simple moments they have the ability to more directly experience their thoughts and feelings.

How does your inability to pay focused attention most negatively impact your emotional well-being? For example, a student once shared that because he was so distracted all the time, he had a hard time paying attention to what he was actually feeling—which caused him to feel increasingly disconnected from himself.

Your ability to focus influences your stress levels and emotional well-being. Being continually distracted is stressful and can make you feel overwhelmed. Be mindful of the environment and activities that support or challenge your ability to focus. Next, let's look at the third aspect of mindful attention: nonjudgmental attention.

Nonjudgmental Attention

Nonjudgmental attention relates to how you emotionally respond to what you're paying attention to. With nonjudgmental attention you are emotionally *nonreactive*, which gives you more freedom to choose how you relate to your thoughts and feelings. For example, you notice a stressful thought or emotion and you don't immediately judge it as good or bad—you just simply observe it.

This ability to nonjudgmentally notice your thoughts and emotions is important to your emotional well-being. That's because it opens a space inside of yourself where you can consciously choose to *respond* based on your goals and values instead of unconsciously *react* based on your immediate emotions.

Can you recall a time when you reacted without choosing your response? What were the consequences (e.g., emotional upset, hurt feelings, behavior that caused harm)? For example, I recently had a conversation with a family member who said something that I thought was pretty lame. Instead of mindfully pausing and choosing my response, I mindlessly reacted and spoke out of irritation. Unfortunately, my mindless words hurt their feelings, caused unnecessary tension, and made me upset with myself because I know I'm capable of responding more skillfully. What about you?

____

____

____

____

Now think of a time when your attention was nonjudgmental, when you were able to simply watch your thoughts and feelings without immediately reacting to them. What was the occasion?

____

____

____

____

How did it feel to be able to observe without reacting? Maybe you felt calm? Relaxed? Clear? Another emotion?

How did your nonjudgmental attention allow you to respond in a way that was more consistent with your goals and values? How did it allow you to *choose* how you wanted to act?

Was there a specific quality to how nonjudgmental attention felt in your body? For example, I often notice that when I practice mindful breathing, I'm more capable of nonjudgmentally observing my thoughts and feelings, which creates an increased sense of openness, spaciousness, and lightness in my mind and body. My jaw releases. The muscles behind my eyes relax. My chest lightens and my shoulders let go. What do you notice in your body?

Are there specific times of day, places, activities, and relationships that tend to make you act reactively? For example, after 8p.m., I tend to be much more judgmental and reactive because I'm tired. In general, HALT (hungry, angry, lonely, tired) states tend to make all of us more likely to be judgmental and reactive.

Times of day when I'm more stressed and reactive...

____

____

____

Places where I'm more stressed and reactive...

____

____

____

Activities that make me more stressed and reactive...

____

____

____

Relationships that make me more stressed and reactive...

____

____

____

Now think about some practical measure you can take to make yourself less reactive in these situations. For example, if you notice you're very reactive the hour before lunch, then maybe you can bring a snack with you to that class.

Practical solutions for stressful times of day...

Practical solutions for stressful places...

Practical solutions for stressful activities...

Practical solutions for stressful relationships...

Are there specific times of day, places, activities, and relationships that help you act more mindfully? For example, many students have noted that when they take walks outside, especially in the morning or evening, it tends to clear their head and allow them to be more open to and less judgmental of their thoughts and feelings. What about you?

Times of day when I'm more mindful...

____

____

____

Places where I'm more mindful...

____

____

____

Activities that make me more mindful...

____

____

____

Relationships that make me more mindful...

____

____

____

Good work. As you develop your mindful breathing practice, continue to pay attention to the circumstances that tend to make you more judgmental and reactive as well as the circumstances that make you more nonjudgmental and mindful.

When you can nonjudgmentally observe your thoughts and feelings, you open a space within yourself where you can choose to act in a manner consistent with your goals and values. Be mindful of the circumstances that tend to be make you most reactive. Conversely, do your best to create the circumstances that allow you to be nonjudgmental.

BIG Idea: In your own words, what's one BIG idea that will stick with you from this activity? In other words, what's an idea that you connected with or that made you think in a new way? Why was it impactful?

Essential Takeaway: Your attention is your window into your experience, so pay attention to your attention. If you want to skillfully manage stress and deepen your emotional well-being, then you need to cultivate mindful attention—attention that is selective, focused, and nonjudgmental. Practicing these qualities of attention will allow you to turn stress into strength.

2

pay attention to your breathing

Your breathing offers the wonderful opportunity to practice mindful attention. Nothing is more essential to your life and emotional well-being than your breathing. In fact, breathing is literally your body's number one priority. Think about it: You can go years without movement, weeks or even months without food, days without water, but only minutes without air. Not to mention, your breathing is deeply connected to your stress levels and emotional experiences from moment to moment. Needless to say, how you breathe is central to your total health and well-being!

Before you start this activity, keep in mind these three tips that will help you get the most out of your breathing practice:

1. Practice this exercise in an environment that is free of clutter, distraction, movement, and noise. If you don't have access to this type of an environment, then find or create the closest thing to it. If you can't find or create it, then practice wherever you are. We'll talk more about

creating an ideal practice environment in section three.

2. Wear loose-fitting clothing that doesn't restrict your ability to breathe, especially around your waist. If you don't have access to this type of clothing, then wear the closest thing to it.
3. If you choose to do this exercise lying down, make sure that you can do so without falling asleep. Sleep is great, but it's doesn't develop the skill of mindful attention. So, if you can lie down and be relaxed and alert, then do it, but if you can't stay alert while lying down, then do these mindful breathing exercises in a seated position.

Here are the instructions for paying attention to your breathing. Read them through, then set aside the book and try doing them. Now, inward we go...

Position: Find a comfortable position where your spine is straight. You can be seated or lying down, assuming, again, that you don't fall asleep.

Hands: To make the sensation of your breath more noticeable, feel free to put your left hand on your chest and your right hand on your lower abdomen. If that's distracting or not comfortable, then allow your hands to be in any comfortable position where they will remain still.

Eyes: Feel free to close your eyes, assuming you won't fall asleep. Having your eyes closed can enhance a sense of calm. If you keep your eyes open, maintain a soft downward gaze at about a 45-degree angle, which would put your gaze about six to seven feet in front of you. Also, keep your eyes still. If you find that your eyes are darting around a lot, it's because your attention is scattered. Again, if you keep your eyes open, try to keep them relaxed and still. If it helps, find an object or spot on the ground to focus them on.

Timer: Set a timer for two minutes. If you want to go longer, go longer. If you want to go shorter, go shorter. For a beginner, two minutes is good, but you can decide what works best for yourself.

Attention: Simply pay attention to the sensation of your breathing for two minutes. Let me be clear: you don't need to think about anything and you don't need to not think about anything. Let your thinking do whatever it wants to do. All you need to do is consciously feel your breathing wherever it is most noticeable. When your attention wanders away from your breathing, gently bring your attention back to your breathing. You will have to do this over and over again—and that's okay. You're training your attention muscle!

When you're done: When the timer goes off and your time is over, try your best to gently and consciously transition out of the exercise. For example, you can take a big breath in and then slowly breathe out. Then you can gently wiggle your toes and fingers. Last, even though it sounds kind of goofy, you can gently pull down and up on your ears. My students love doing this because it's silly and very relaxing all at once.

Okay, good luck. I know you can do this. I'll be right here when you're done.

Ready, set, start the timer ... go!

Two minutes later...

You made it! Nice work. Take a moment to be proud of yourself...

Now, before you fall back into your distracted "everyday mind," I want you write down your initial thoughts about the exercise. In one word, describe how it felt to do this exercise.

Your word: _____

In general, was the exercise easy or difficult for you? Were you able to effortlessly stay with your breathing? Or was your mind like a squirrel running across a busy street?

What were some thoughts that you noticed during the exercise?

What were some feelings that you noticed during the exercise? Where in your body did you feel them?

If your attention wandered from your breathing during the exercise, where did it wander to?

If it was very difficult for you to keep your attention on your breathing, try the same exercise again but with this adjustment (and feel free to try this version of the exercise even if you had no difficulties the first time around): Everything from the first exercise stays the same, except this time I want you to use your finger to trace along this oval while you're breathing.

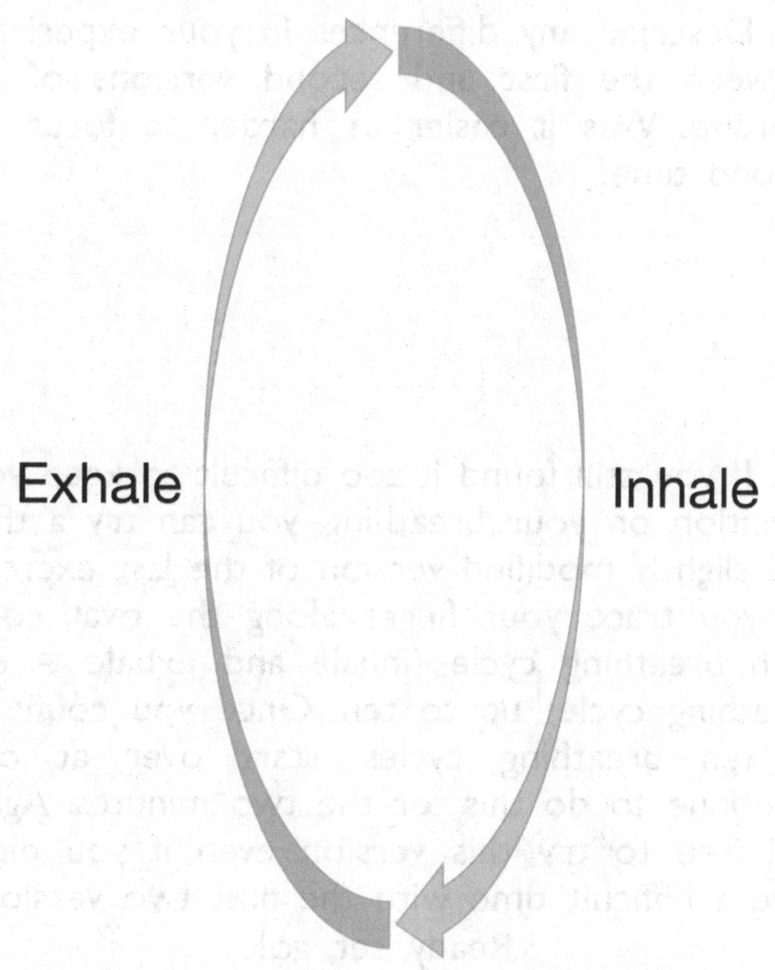

- As you breathe in, follow the arrows of the "inhale" and trace your finger downward on the oval (toward you).
- As you breathe out, follow the arrows of the "exhale" and trace your finger upward on the oval (away from you).

Okay, now give it a shot.

Bravo!

Describe any differences in your experience between the first and second versions of the exercise. Was it easier or harder to focus the second time?

____

____

____

____

If you still found it too difficult to keep your attention on your breathing, you can try a third and slightly modified version of the last exercise: As you trace your finger along the oval, count each breathing cycle (inhale and exhale = one breathing cycle) up to ten. Once you count up to ten breathing cycles, start over at one. Continue to do this for the two minutes. Again, feel free to try this version even if you didn't have a difficult time with the first two versions.

Ready, set, go!

Two minutes later...

Okay, nice job.

Again, describe any differences in how it felt to do this version of the exercise compared to the first or second version. Was it easier to focus? Harder?

____

____

____

____

Continue to practice any of the three versions of this exercise until you feel that you're able to keep your attention on your breathing for *most* of the two minutes. Once you're able to do this, then incrementally extend the period of time to keep challenging yourself.

BIG Idea: In your own words, what's one BIG idea that will stick with you from this activity? In other words, what's an idea that you connected with or that made you think in a new way? Why was it impactful?

____

____

____

____

Essential Takeaway: Learning to skillfully manage your attention begins with an awareness of your breathing. Create a clean, calm, and quiet place to practice. Wear clothing that doesn't restrict your breathing. Find a comfortable position—upright or lying down—that allows you to be relaxed but alert. Start with two minutes of paying attention to the sensation of your breathing wherever it is most vivid for you. The more you practice, the easier it will get to focus your attention, and the more skillfully you'll be able to manage your stress by simply noticing it nonjudgmentally.

3

feel and relax your body

In the last activity, you learned to pay attention to your breathing. In this exercise, called the body scan, you're going to use an awareness of breathing to feel into your body as a whole. Bodily awareness is an important skill because it helps offset the human tendency to get lost in thought. Sometimes, when you're lost in the drama of your own anxious thinking, you forget that you're living in a body. So, let's now use your breathing as a guide into and through the vast world of bodily sensation so that you can deepen your connection to the present moment through an increased awareness of your body.

Find a comfortable position. You can sit up straight in a chair or lie down on the ground. If you're sitting, allow your hands to rest comfortably in your lap. If you're lying down, allow your hands to fall to your sides with your palms open and facing up.

What posture works best for you? Why?

____

____

Shut or relax your eyes. Close your eyes or look downward with a soft gaze at a

45-degree angle. Which feels more comfortable for you: eyes closed or eyes open? Describe what each one feels like:

Eyes closed: ____________________

____

Eyes open with a soft downward gaze:

____

Breathe through your nose. Bring your attention to your breathing. If you can, close your mouth and breathe only through your nose. If you want to make the sensation of breathing more distinct, put one hand on your belly and the other hand on your chest. Don't change your breathing—just simply feel it. Continue to feel your breath for two minutes.

How does it feel to breathe only through your nose?

____

____

Feel your body. Now that you've established a connection with your breath, spend a minute or so noticing all the sensations in your body: What does it feel like to be in your body right now? Circle any that apply:

Tight	Open	Free	Closed	Relaxed	Tense
Heavy	Light	Numb	Clear	Quiet	Noisy

Add any words that aren't listed: _______

____

Are there areas of your body that you notice more than others? If so, where?

Are there areas of your body that you notice less? If so, where?

Are there areas of your body that you don't notice at all? If so, where?

Feel your feet. Now that you've anchored your awareness in your breath, expand your awareness of breath into an awareness of your body as a whole. Start by bringing attention to your feet. Notice any sensations around your feet. Feel free to wiggle your toes to stimulate sensation. As you feel the sensations all around your feet, continue to feel your breath. If you can't feel anything, pay attention to what feeling nothing feels like (yes, that sounds odd, but try it!).

What sensations do you notice in your feet?

Feel your legs. Continue to feel your breathing and your feet. When you're ready, expand your attention up to and around your ankles, shins, calves, knees, thighs, and hamstrings. Notice the richness of sensations throughout your legs. If you notice any tension, tightness, or pain, notice it without judgment. If your attention drifts during this exercise, gently bring it back—again, without judgment—to your breathing and then to the sensations in your body.

What sensation do you notice in your legs?

If your attention drifts into thinking, gently invite it back to the sensations of your breathing and the sensations of your body.

Feel your back. As you continue to feel your breath, feet, and legs, now slowly open your awareness more and notice the sensations in your hips up though your lower back. Take a moment to breathe, letting go of tension or judgments that might arise. Now, slowly expand your awareness from your hips and lower back up to your middle and upper back, noticing all of the sensations there, noticing any contact with your chair if you're sitting or the ground if you're lying down.

What sensations do you notice in your back?

Feel your belly. Continue to feel your breath. Continue to feel your toes, feet, legs, hips, and back. Now, expand your awareness to your abdomen, noticing any sounds or movement inside your belly. Notice the sensation of clothing resting on your skin. Notice the rising and falling of your belly with each breath. If your attention wanders or if you find yourself lost in judgment about anything you're experiencing, gently bring your attention back to your breathing and all the sensations of your body.

What sensations do you notice in your belly?

____

____

Feel your chest. Continue to feel your breathing and your body. Now, expand your awareness from the belly to the chest. Notice if you can feel your heartbeat. Notice your chest rise and fall as your lungs fill and empty. If any tension, tightness, or judgment arises in your awareness, simply notice it without judgment and return to the sensations of your breathing and your body.

What sensations do you notice in your chest?

____

____

Feel your arms. As you exhale, expand your awareness down your arms to your hands, fingers, and fingertips, and feel the richness of sensations arising. Notice, without judgment, if your arms feel different from one another—or if one hand feels warmer or colder than the other. Notice if there's a finger that is most vivid in your mind's eye. And, then, notice your breathing and all the sensations of your whole body below the neck.

What sensations do you notice in your arms?

____

____

Feel your shoulders, neck, and throat. Continue to notice your breath, and now expand your awareness to the neck, shoulders, and throat. Notice the trickle of air moving through the back of your throat. Notice the gravity of the shoulders falling toward the floor. Without judgment, notice any tension and simply continue to breathe and feel your body as a whole.

What sensations do you notice in your shoulders, neck, and throat?

____

____

Feel your face and scalp. On the next exhale, expand your awareness to your face and scalp. Notice the abundance of sensations there: the sensations around your closed lips; the stream of air entering and exiting your nose; the tickle of sensation at the tip of your nose; and the delicate pressure around, behind, and between your eyes. Now, expand your awareness around your scalp and all the way up to the crown of your head.

What sensations do you notice in your face and scalp?

Feel your whole body breathe. Now, feel your breath fill every corner of your body and every cell of your being. There's nowhere you need to go, nothing you need to do, and no one you need to be. Let it all go. Feel all the sensations of your body—from head to fingertip to toe—ebb and flow with the rhythm of your breath. Stay in this place of open bodily awareness for as long as you can. When your attention wanders, invite it back home to your breath, to your body, and allow yourself to be nourished by the life-giving energy of your breath.

What sensations do you notice throughout your whole body?

Mindfully transition into your day. Whenever you're ready to move on with your day, do so, but be mindful of your transition out of this activity. After you spend time cultivating a deeper awareness of your breathing and your body, you may find that you immediately jump back into your distracted "everyday mind" when the exercise is over. When you do this, you lose that deeper quality of awareness that allowed you to relax and connect with yourself. To prevent this from happening, think of the transition out of this exercise as a continuation of the exercise itself. Bring this deeper awareness of your breathing and your body with you into your next activity and throughout your day.

Now that you've finished the body scan, what does it feel like to be in your body? Circle any that apply:

Tight	Open	Free	Closed	Relaxed	Tense
Heavy	Light	Numb	Clear	Quiet	Noisy

Add any words that aren't listed: ______

______

Does your body feel different now compared to before the body scan? If so, describe how in detail.

______

______

______

______

BIG Idea: In your own words, what's one BIG idea that will stick with you from this activity? In other words, what's an idea that you connected with or that made you think in a new way? Why was it impactful?

______

______

Essential Takeaway: When you get lost in your head, you lose connection with your body and to the present moment. By reestablishing an awareness of your body through the breath, you can stay connected the moment stress and anxiety try to drag you into the past or push you into the future. Always remember, no matter how lost you think you are, your breathing and your body are always right here, right now, calling you home.

4

know your emotions through your breathing

Because your emotions and breathing are so deeply connected, when you pay attention to your breathing, you're also paying attention to your emotions, to how you feel inside. In fact, how you feel in every moment is expressed in and regulated by your breathing.

Sometimes when you get stressed out and overwhelmed by difficult emotions, it's hard to get a handle on these difficult emotions because you don't have a direct access point to them. In those moments when you feel overwhelmed, it feels like the strong emotion is everywhere, but nowhere specifically—which can make you feel even more overwhelmed.

This is exactly why mindful breathing is so important: it's a direct access point to what you're feeling in every moment. Your breathing never lies! As you sit here right now, take a moment to notice your breathing: What are the qualities of your breathing in this moment? Circle the words that apply:

Light	Slow	Relaxed	Quiet	Effortless	Deep
Heavy	Fast	Tense	Loud	Difficult	Shallow

Can you describe what you're feeling emotionally right now? Finish this sentence: *I am feeling...*

Write your emotion here: _____

Now look at the words you circled above to describe how your breathing feels and compare them to the emotion you wrote. Do you see any connections between the words you circled to describe how your breathing felt and your emotional state? If you mostly circled words from the top line, then you're likely feeling relaxed and calm. If you mostly circled words from the bottom line, then you're likely feeling stressed and anxious.

What connection did you notice between the qualities of your breathing and your emotional state? For example, students often notice that when their breathing is heavy, rapid, or shallow, their emotional state is stressed out and anxious. What do you notice?

____

____

____

____

Developing emotional awareness through an awareness of your breathing is important because the better you get at it, the more you'll notice changes in your breathing before you notice changes in your emotion. This is essential for your well-being because, especially with difficult emotions like anxiety, often by the time you notice what you're feeling, it's already overwhelmed you—and at that point, it can be hard to redirect that state. As the old saying goes, "An ounce of prevention is worth a pound of cure!" *So notice small changes in your breathing before you experience big changes in your emotions.*

Here's an exercise to try over the course of a day. Schedule a few times of day when you can stop and notice how you're feeling by noticing how you're breathing. Here are the steps:

Step 1: Schedule three times a day when you will check in with your breathing for one minute—for example, when you wake up, at noon, and in the evening (just set alarms on your phone).

Step 2: During this one-minute breathing check-in, all you need to do is sit upright and still, close your eyes, put your right hand on your belly and your left hand on your chest, and simply pay attention to the qualities of your breathing.

Step 3: When your minute is up, write down a one- to three-word description of the qualities you noticed in that moment. For example, you might write "calm," "anxious," or "excited and hopeful."

The big idea here is to develop more awareness of how your breathing communicates your emotion.

For one week, record the results of your daily breathing check-in. Here is a form you can use for Monday. Then go to the website for this book, http://www.newharbinger.com/47247, and download a worksheet that you can save and use for the rest of the week (see the very back of this book for more details).

Daily Breathing Check-In

Day: **Monday**

Morning breathing check-in:

I noticed that my breathing was...

Light	Shallow	Relaxed	Restrict-ed	Effort-less	Loud	Deep
Heavy	Slow	Tense	Quiet	Difficult	Open	Fast

I noticed that emotionally I was feeling...

____

____

____

Midday breathing check-in:

I noticed that my breathing was...

Light	Shallow	Relaxed	Restrict-ed	Effort-less	Loud	Deep
Heavy	Slow	Tense	Quiet	Difficult	Open	Fast

I noticed that emotionally I was feeling...

Evening breathing check-in:

I noticed that my breathing was...

Light	Shallow	Relaxed	Restrict-ed	Effort-less	Loud	Deep
Heavy	Slow	Tense	Quiet	Difficult	Open	Fast

I noticed that emotionally I was feeling...

Researchers have found that just the simple act of noticing your breathing, of consciously breathing, regulates your emotions.[3] So, none of this has to be complicated—just pay attention to your breathing and use it as an indicator of your emotional state in any given moment.

BIG Idea: In your own words, what's one BIG idea that will stick with you from this activity? In other words, what's an idea that you connected with or that made you think in a new way? Why was it impactful?

Essential Takeaway: Your breathing and your emotions are deeply connected. Sometimes it's hard to tell what you actually feel because feelings can be fluid and hard to pinpoint. Your breathing, on the other hand, never lies. It's a straightforward status report on your emotional state. By learning to pay mindful attention to your breathing, you can develop greater self-awareness of what you're feeling—which empowers you to act skillfully in the face of stress.

5

notice your breathing to experience your surroundings

One of the most common features of being stressed out is that we lose awareness of our surroundings. This is because we lose awareness of the body. And we lose awareness of the body because we lose awareness of the breath.

Why is this a big deal? It's a big deal because when you stop paying attention to your breath, body, and surroundings, your thoughts and emotions exclusively define your experience. This is a dangerous place to be because when you can't see beyond your thoughts and emotions, they're likely controlling your life.

For example, you're in the middle of world civ. class, and suddenly you feel very anxious. In fact, you feel an overwhelming sense that you need to get up and run out of the classroom. In this moment, if you don't mindfully breathe, notice the sensations in your body away from where you're feeling the anxiety (like the tops of your hands and the bottoms of your feet), and notice the details of your classroom (like the decorations on the walls, the color of the floor, the temperature of the room, the feel and texture of the desk, the smell of the air, and so on), you'll likely get swept away by racing thoughts and anxiety and run out of the room. Again, when you can't see beyond your thoughts and feelings, you'll act according to them.

Now, let's show how using mindful breathing to pay attention to your body and surroundings can transform the anxiety-attack situation above.

You're in the middle of world civ. class, and suddenly you feel very anxious. In fact, you feel an overwhelming sense that you need to get up and run out of the classroom.

- In this moment, you immediately bring your attention to your breathing and consciously slow it down.
- As you notice your breathing and slow it down, you also feel into the parts of your body farthest away from the sensations of anxiety (which are usually in the chest and head), like the bottoms of your feet.
- As you expand your awareness of your body by consciously feeling the sensations in it, you also notice the details of your surroundings, like the posters of ancient Greece on the wall, the pale beige color of the linoleum-tiled floor, the cool temperature of the room, the scent of cleaning supplies mixed with an

overpowering potpourri air freshener, and the smooth feeling of your desk.

By mindfully paying attention to all of these details of your experience, you're able to expand the spotlight of attention and see clearly that there's more happening on the stage of your experience in this moment than racing thoughts and nagging feelings of stress and anxiety.

Okay, it's your turn. Identify a time in your life when the spotlight of your attention narrowed down to one thought or emotion on the stage of your experience because you were anxious and distressed. For example, maybe you earned a bad grade on an exam and all you could think about the stress and anxiety this caused you. First, briefly describe what happened:

____

____

____

____

Can you remember what happened to your breathing during this event? (Refer to the qualities listed in activity 4, if you'd like.)

____

____

What did you feel in your body and where did you feel it?

____

____

What happened to your awareness of your surroundings? Did you consciously notice them? Or was your attention spotlight narrowed to what you were thinking and feeling?

Now, let's do a virtual simulation of that same experience, except now you're going to expand the spotlight of attention by doing the following:

- Consciously feel your breathing and slow it down.
- Feel the sensations of your body, especially the areas of the body farthest from the feelings of the thought or emotion.
- Use your five senses (sight, sound, smell, taste, and touch) to notice the details of your surroundings.

First, take a minute or two, close your eyes, do nothing, and relax into a comfortable position.

Now, replay the event in your mind, but envision how it might have played out had you more mindfully noticed your breath, body, and surroundings. Describe how the event might have played out.

Look at the two descriptions you wrote about the event: how it actually played out and how it could've played out had you been more mindful. What's the biggest difference between the two? For example, how did you think, feel, speak, and act differently in the two descriptions?

How did an awareness of your breath, body, and surroundings contribute to the difference you described?

BIG Idea: In your own words, what's one BIG idea that will stick with you from this activity? In other words, what's an idea that you connected with or that made you think in a new way? Why was it impactful?

Essential Takeaway: Too often, when you're stressed, it's easy to get lost in your thoughts and emotions. A skillful way to correct this tendency is to feel the breath, which is to feel the body, which is to feel and notice your surroundings. Connecting attention to the breath, breath to the body, and the body to its surroundings helps bring *all of you* back to where life is actually happening: *the present moment.*

Section One Reflection

Yeehaw! Section one is done. Good work. You have learned a lot about mindful breathing. So, take a moment to bring it all together. I'll give you a refresher:

- Pay attention to what you pay attention to and how you pay attention—aim for mindful attention that is selective, focused, and nonjudgmental.
- Pay attention to your breathing—it's connected to everything you feel.
- Pay attention to your body—it's always in the present (even though your mind isn't).
- Pay attention to how your emotions influence your breathing—your breathing is your mind made visible.
- Pay attention to your surroundings—they're a counterweight to your tendency to get lost in your thoughts and emotions.

Describe what was most impactful from section one.

____

____

How might this change what you do moving forward?

____

____

SECTION TWO

Use Your Breathing to Manage Your Emotional Stress

Whether you like it or not, stress is a reality of life that you can't escape. This might sound disheartening, but it's not. Without stress, you can't learn, change, adapt, and evolve toward greater emotional intelligence and freedom. The inescapability of stress is actually a call to action: learn to skillfully utilize stress for positive adaptation and growth. So, let's get busy then transforming your stress into emotional strength!

6

measure your breathing to assess your stress levels

Each day, you use things like phones, computers, and cars, but just because you can *use* these things doesn't mean that you *know how they work*. What I mean is that you can drive a car, for instance, without knowing how the car actually works. Similarly, you drive your physiology without actually understanding what's going on "underneath the hood." The more mindful you are of the signs that your physiology is redlining, the more successfully you can perform preventative maintenance—like mindful breathing—so that your "engine" doesn't break down.

Changes in your breathing are the first sign of stress—your breathing changes in real time to help your physiology adjust to increasing levels of stress. So, let's learn to identify how your breathing can tell you what's going on under the hood before your physiology goes up in smoke.

How Fast Are You Breathing?

First and foremost, stress makes you breathe faster. This is because when the stress switch gets flipped in your brain, your body needs more energy, and oxygen is your primary source of energy. Oxygen is a vital aspect of your body's energy system, and your physiology constantly and closely monitors it in relation to your energy demands. When your breathing rate is elevated while your body is at rest, this is similar to a car engine revving while in neutral.

Let's evaluate your breathing rate. In this exercise, you'll time your breathing for one minute. Don't do this test while you're exercising, right after you've exercised, or while you're active in any way. You should be in a normal, at-rest state. You'll need a stopwatch (available on your phone) for this exercise.

When you're ready, start the stopwatch and count how many times you breathe in one minute. Inhaling and then exhaling is considered one breath. Don't try to control your breathing or change it in any way. Just breathe as normally as you can.

Write your score (i.e., number of breaths) here: _____

Now, do the same thing one more time so you have two scores to compare.

Write your second score here: _____

If your scores are drastically different (by more than five breaths per minute), then do the test a third time.

Write your third score here: _____

The normal range is twelve to twenty breaths per minute. Twenty to twenty-five breaths per minute suggests that your breathing rate is elevated and your system is stressed, and above twenty-five breaths per minute at rest is considered atypical.

If your breathing rate is twenty-five or more breaths per minute, keep retesting it for a few days to make sure this score is consistent. If under normal circumstances you're consistently breathing twenty-five or more times per minute, it's likely that your physiology is under a lot of stress, and I'd recommend that you ask your doctor about it. This stress could be due to emotional and/or physical factors. An example of emotional stress is being upset about school, friends, or family. An example of physical stress is consistently having too much or too little physical activity or having respiratory issues, such as asthma or allergies.

Even though you might make a distinction between emotional stress and physical stress, your physiology doesn't make any distinctions between them. From the perspective of your physiology, stress is stress. It's all the same. Your breathing rate shows how hard your body is working to supply energy (oxygen). If your body is working hard to supply energy, that shows an elevated demand for energy—which is by definition "stress."

Let's put this into context. Going back to the car engine analogy, breathing too much at rest is like sitting in your car at a stoplight with your foot on the gas, revving your engine while the car isn't moving. It's not good for the car to work too hard at rest, and this is exactly what you're doing when you're overbreathing at rest. Pay attention to your breathing rate, and when you notice your breathing becoming faster than normal, use that as a cue to slow down, rest, and recover.

Time Your Carbon Dioxide Tolerance

For this exercise, you're going to do the exercise first, and then I'll explain it afterward. Okay, here's what you need to do (don't begin until after you read the note below step 3):

Step 1: Get a stopwatch (on your phone).

Step 2: Close your mouth and breathe through your nose at a normal rate for about a minute.

Step 3: After a minute, and after an exhale, pinch your nose closed and time how long you can hold your breath until you notice the *first distinct feeling* that you need to breathe. Once you feel the first sign of needing to breathe, stop timing, and that's your score.

Note: You're *not* timing how long you can hold your breath. Instead, you're timing how long it takes to feel the first distinct sign that you need to breathe. There's a difference. Even though you could hold your breath longer, you're not going to because that's not the point of this exercise. Here's the best way to know if you've done it correctly: if you're gasping for air after you stop the timer, you held your breath too long. You should be able to resume normal breathing when you're done.

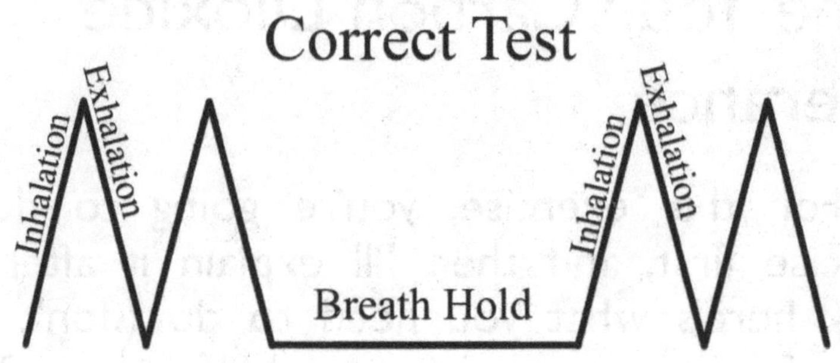

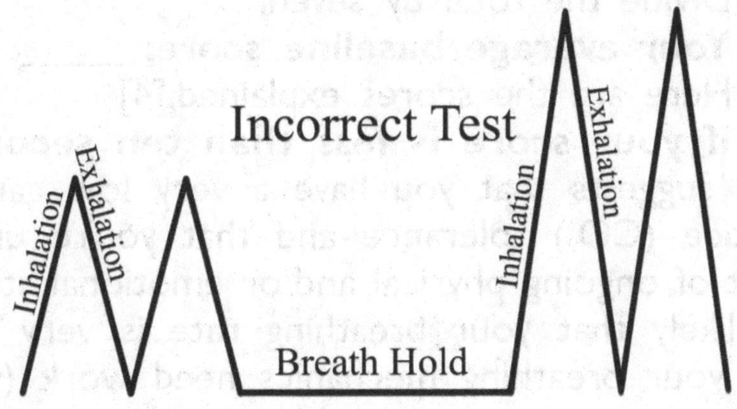

Okay, now do the exercise and write your time here: _____

Do this test seven days in a row (ideally when you first wake up), record your scores, and average them over time (at least a week). You'll get better at doing the exercise the more you do it and will, therefore, get a more accurate sense of your baseline score. So, moving forward, don't base everything on just one or two test scores.

Sunday morning score: _____
Monday morning score: _____
Tuesday morning score: _____
Wednesday morning score: _____
Thursday morning score: _____
Friday morning score: _____
Saturday morning score: _____

Now calculate your baseline by adding up each of the seven daily scores above and then dividing the total by seven.

Your seven-day total: _____

Divide the total by seven.

Your average baseline score: ____

Here are the scores explained.[4]

If your score is less than ten seconds: This suggests that you have a very low carbon dioxide (CO_2) tolerance and that you're under a lot of ongoing physical and/or emotional stress. It's likely that your breathing rate is very high and your breathing mechanics need work (we'll discuss more about breathing mechanics later). With a score this low, it's also possible that you have an underlying respiratory condition, like asthma or chronic allergies. The lower your score, the worse your symptoms probably are. A score in this range just means that you're really lucky to be reading this workbook right now—and that you have the opportunity to improve!

In my personal experience administering this test, I rarely encounter someone who is under five seconds. If your score is consistently under five seconds, and it cannot be explained by a respiratory condition like asthma, it could be due to something emotionally stressful you've experienced or chronically elevated levels of stress. If this is the case, I highly encourage you to talk to someone you can trust, ideally a medical doctor, social worker, and/or counselor.

If your score is consistently between ten and twenty seconds: This indicates that you probably have a lower tolerance to CO_2, a fair amount of stress, a higher breathing rate, and less-than-ideal breathing mechanics. Though it's not as severe as under ten seconds, it still suggests that you should address underlying physical and/or emotional stress for optimal health. Luckily for you, you can improve your breathing with the exercises in this workbook!

If your score is consistently between twenty and forty seconds: You're in a better place. Twenty to thirty seconds is an average score and suggests that you're not excessively physically and/or emotionally stressed. Thirty to forty seconds suggests good emotional and physical health. Your breathing rate is likely lower and your mechanics are sound. But don't be too comfortable with this range of scores because you can do even better!

If your score is consistently greater than forty seconds: You have a good CO_2 tolerance and you are likely physically fit and emotionally balanced. It's also likely that your breathing rate is lower because your physiology is efficiently using oxygen. The higher your score is above forty seconds, the more you may tend to be physically and emotionally tolerant of stress and the lower your breathing rate per minute likely is.

It's important to recognize that just because your CO_2 tolerance is okay right now doesn't mean it won't shift for the worse if you become chronically stressed out and anxious. This is why consistently doing this assessment helps you better recognize what's going on in your physiology before you would otherwise be conscious of it. We'll talk about how to improve your CO_2 tolerance in section three.

BIG Idea: In your own words, what's one BIG idea that will stick with you from this activity? In other words, what's an idea that you connected with or that made you think in a new way? Why was it impactful?

____

____

____

____

Essential Takeaway: As you learn how to better read and use your physiology, you'll ensure that you'll see and respond to the "check engine" light on the dashboard of your mind before your emotional well-being goes up in smoke. Don't wait until stress and anxiety get the best of you before you take action. Be proactive and learn how to better read and understand what your physiology tells you through your breathing rate and CO_2 tolerance in real time.

7

be mindful of your stress bucket

Stress sets off the rapid breathing and low CO_2 tolerance that we explored in the last activity. Stress, then, would seem to be the root of the problem—but since stress is an unavoidable part of life (after all, you need some stress to stay healthy, learn, and grow), what are you left to do? Are you just doomed to stress, fast breathing, poor CO_2 tolerance, and emotional upheaval?

No, you're not doomed. All you need is the power of mindful attention and breathing. If you increase awareness of how your breathing reveals your stress, you can take back control before your breathing and stress go into a tailspin! So, let's work on and develop your stress-awareness skills to help you control your breathing and, ultimately, your emotional responses.

Your Stress Bucket

It's important to remember that some stress is good because without it you won't be alert enough to pay close attention to the important things in life that you need to do. So, what you want is the right blend of alertness and calm. Too much alertness and you're over stressed and hyper focused. Too much calm and you're drowsy and inattentive. Think of it as a continuum, where sleep is the lowest state of arousal, and an anxiety attack is the highest state of arousal. The sweet spot is somewhere in the middle.

Let's imagine that your stress level is water in a bucket. You measure the stress level on a scale of 1 to 10:

- A little stress in the bucket is a 1, which means almost asleep (an empty bucket would be 0, representing deep sleep or unconsciousness).
- On the other end of the scale, a completely filled bucket is a 10 (high stress). An overflowing bucket is high stress or an anxiety meltdown.
- A half-filled bucket is a 5, which is actually where you need to be to do most of the important activities in your daily life. A 5 is just the right blend of calm and alertness (think of activities you enjoy doing: talking to friends, riding a bike, gaming, driving a car, and so on. All of these activities require a blend of alertness and calm).

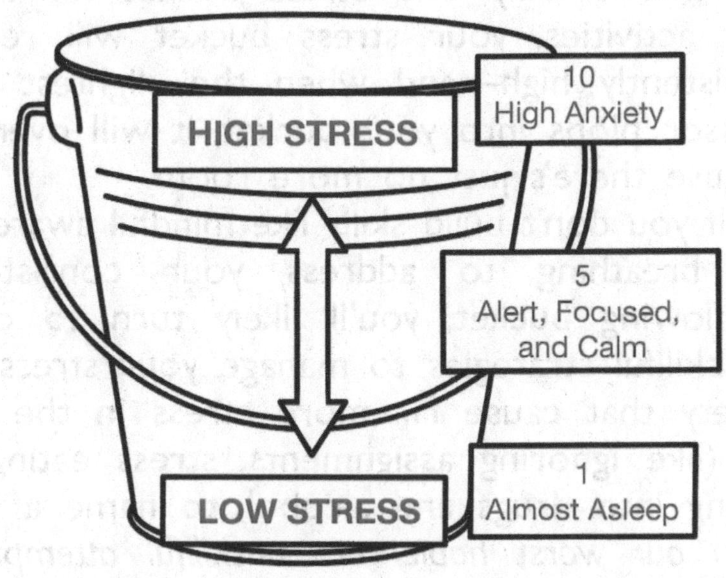

Based on this 1–10 scale, how full is your bucket right now?

Write your score here: _____.

Good, now hold on to that score for a moment.

In your mind, you likely divide how you spend your time into different buckets. For example, you have a school bucket, a baseball or jazz band bucket, a friend bucket, a family bucket, an entertainment bucket, and a social media bucket. You get the idea. This is called "compartmentalizing."

Unfortunately, for all of us, our physiologies don't care how we mentally compartmentalize the different parts of our lives. Your physiology is your only "bucket," and all the stress from your daily activities fills it up. If you don't realize that there's only one stress bucket for all of your activities, your stress bucket will remain consistently high—and when the slightest little stressor plops into your bucket, it will overflow because there's just no more room.

If you don't build skills like mindful awareness and breathing to address your consistently overflowing bucket, you'll likely turn to other less skillful strategies to manage your stress and anxiety that cause far more stress in the long run (like ignoring assignments, stress eating, or getting into drugs and alcohol, to name a few). *Often our worst habits are unskillful attempts to manage our stress bucket levels.* More on this in a moment.

You already picked a number for how full your stress bucket is right now. Next, label the different hoses that fill up your stress bucket to that level. For example, if your bucket was at a 7, what are the major hoses (stressors) that fill your bucket up to that level? Label the five main hoses that fill your bucket (if you want, you can add some additional hoses if you have more).

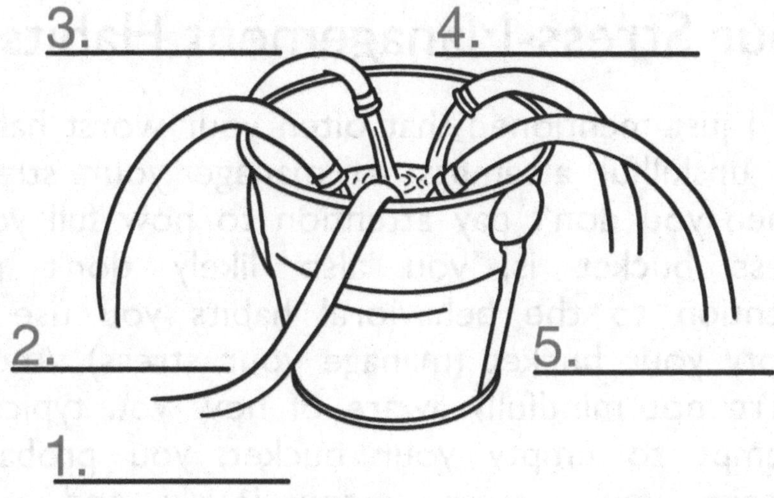

Now that you've labeled the different hoses that fill your bucket, identify which hoses pour the most stress into your bucket. List from 1 (the most stress) to 5 (the least stress), and then estimate how much of your total stress each hose contributes (for example, 10% or 50%).

Rank	Percentage of total stress
1.	%
2.	%
3.	%
4.	%
5.	%

Your Stress-Management Habits

I just mentioned that often your worst habits are unskillful attempts to manage your stress. When you don't pay attention to how full your stress bucket is, you also likely don't pay attention to the behavioral habits you use to empty your bucket (manage your stress). And if you're not mindfully aware of how you typically attempt to empty your bucket, you probably manage your stress unconsciously and with behaviors that do not support your health and emotional well-being in the long run—which means that they just actually fill your bucket up more!

It's also worth mentioning here that distraction is not the same thing as relaxation. We often use things like food, phones, video games, sleeping, and socializing as distractions to wind down and throw our brains into neutral. For example, even though playing around on your phone distracts you from other things in your day-today life, it's not actually allowing your bucket to drain—which means that it's actually just another hose pouring into your stress bucket. And since many of us are on our phones *a lot*, we often don't realize that this unconscious behavior steadily pours stress into our bucket all day long—which can wear us down and make us less resilient in the face of additional stress.

Here's a list of common distractions and "bad habits" people often turn to as an unskillful way to empty their stress buckets. Circle the ones that you engage in.

- eating too much or too little
- working too much
- avoiding responsibilities
- spending money/buying things
- sleeping too much or too little
- exercising too much or too little
- playing video games
- spending too much time on social media
- drinking alcohol or taking drugs (recreational, prescription, and/or over the counter)
- withdrawing from socializing or oversocializing

Even though these behaviors might provide a short-term distraction from stress, they actually cause more long-term stress and problems—because (a) they don't actually lower the stress level in your bucket, (b) they add more stress to it, or (c) they make you more likely to have a full bucket in the future!

You might wonder what makes a good habit "good" and a bad habit "bad." It has to do with the effect it has on your *baseline happiness* (how happy you tend to be in general) and your well-being. When you're considering the value of a habit, consider the following three questions:

1. Does the habit *increase* my baseline happiness and well-being?

2. Does the habit *decrease* my baseline happiness and well-being?
3. Does the habit *maintain* my current baseline happiness and well-being?

For example, if every time I got stressed out, I made myself a bowl of ice cream, I would likely be lowering my baseline happiness and well-being and adding more stress to my bucket. Once my bowl is empty, my sense of relief and satisfaction will be gone. I'll soon realize that I'm just as stressed as before, and I might even start to criticize myself for eating ice cream again. These emotional consequences will be compounded by the physical consequences of eating ice cream all the time. When you consider all of these things, it's obvious that eating ice cream is not my best stress-management option because it clearly lowers my baseline happiness and well-being, jeopardizes my health, and leaves my bucket closer to overfilling.

Now it's your turn. List five unskillful or "bad" stress-management habits and then fill out the other three columns. I did the first one to give you an example.

Bad Stress-Management Habit	Lowers Your Stress Bucket in the Moment?	Makes You Happy and Well in the Future?	Increases, Decreases, or Maintains Baseline?
Eating cereal at 10 p.m. (My bad habit ☺)	Not really. Just briefly relaxes me. Makes my brain feel numb and sleepy.	Nope. Definitely not. I sleep less well and wake up tired and hungrier because I ate late at night.	Decreases. Not a ton, but enough for me to realize that it's not an ideal habit for lowering my stress bucket levels.
1.			
2.			
3.			
4.			
5.			

Pay attention to your stress-management habits. Even though they might work in the moment, they often have hidden consequences that end up making you feel more stressed and less well. Because we always have our phones in hand, many of us use them to distract ourselves from our stress and anxiety. But remember, distraction is not relaxation. Even though your attention is temporarily absorbed in social media, your underlying stress levels are not going down. So, next time you reach for your phone when you're stressed, take a mindful moment, feel your breathing, and slow down.

Emptying Your Stress Bucket

When your stress bucket is getting full, what are five skillful or "good" stress-management habits that will actually increase your baseline happiness and well-being and lower your stress?

Here's a list of common good habits people often turn to as a skillful way to empty their stress buckets. Circle the ones that you utilize:

- practicing mindful breathing
- stretching
- eating healthy, nutrient-dense foods
- taking a break
- making to-do lists
- practicing gratitude
- resting/sleeping when needed
- exercising the right amount
- making a meaningful social connection
- reading, writing, drawing, or doing anything creative
- performing random acts of kindness

Fill out the columns. I did the first one to give you an example.

Good Stress-Management Habit	Lowers Your Stress in the Moment?	Makes You Happy and Well in the Future?	Increases, Decreases, or Maintains Baseline?
Mindful Breathing	Absolutely. By breathing consciously and slowly, I can lower my stress within minutes.	Yes. Because it gives me confidence that I have the ability to influence and change stressful feelings.	Increases. Because I have confidence that I can manage my stress bucket, I have confidence that I can take on challenging tasks—like writing this workbook!
1.			
2.			
3.			
4.			
5.			

Excellent work. By increasing your awareness of your stress bucket, you can become more conscious of what fills it up and be more skillful with how you lower it back down!

BIG Idea: In your own words, what's one BIG idea that will stick with you from this activity? In other words, what's an idea that you connected with or that made you think in a new way? Why was it impactful?

Essential Takeaway: Be mindful of your stress bucket. Knowing where your stress levels are empowers you to proactively and skillfully manage your stress. If you're not paying attention to how full your stress bucket is, then you're likely also not paying attention to how to attempt to manage your stress. Remember that often our worst habits are unskillful attempts to manage our stress. Unskillful stress-management strategies might offer temporary relief in the moment, but they often just add to your stress later. Choose strategies, like mindful breathing, that help you chill out now and later.

8

pay attention to what your breathing and your body tell you

When I ask students how they know how full their stress buckets are, they initially say things like "I just know I'm at a 7." And then I ask them, "But how do you know? Based on what?" Then they look at me confused, and I explain that whether they're conscious of it or not, their stress-level awareness is breathing awareness. Through an awareness of the presence or absence of tension in your breathing, you can begin to identify and redirect rising stress levels before they overfill your bucket and drown your emotional well-being.

As I already mentioned, your emotional stress and the quality of your breathing are deeply connected. So, let's take a moment to observe and examine characteristics of your breathing more closely.

> **Step 1:** Sit up straight—a straight spine is an alert mind! Or, if it's more comfortable, lie flat on your back.

Step 2: Once you've found a comfortable position that allows your spine to be straight, put one hand on your belly and one hand on your chest.

Step 3: For roughly one to two minutes, simply notice your breathing. Don't change it, just observe it. Pay close attention to what your breathing communicates about your emotional state.

Once you've established a conscious awareness of your breathing after a minute or two, fill out this breathing assessment that addresses—on a scale of 1 to 10—three different qualities of your breathing: weight, rate, and depth.

Breathing Weight

Light 1 2 3 4 5 6 7 8 9 10 Heavy

Breathing Rate

Slow 1 2 3 4 5 6 7 8 9 10 Fast

Breathing Depth

Deep 1 2 3 4 5 6 7 8 9 10 Shallow

Now add the three scores up and divide them by 3. For example, if you had 7, 6, and 8, you would add them up, and the total would equal 21. Then you'd divide 21 by 3, which equals 7.

Score #1 _____+ Score #2 _____+ Score #3 = Total

Total _____ divided by 3 = _____

Now that you've assessed these three qualities of your breathing and calculated an average score, let's briefly talk about the scales. The three qualities on the right of the scales (heavy, rapid, and shallow) are sensations associated with a full stress bucket. On the other hand, the three qualities on the left of the scales (light, slow, and deep) are sensations associated with an empty stress bucket, deep relaxation, and sleep.

In doing this assessment with hundreds of my students, I've observed a few patterns:

- If you score high on one of the qualities, you likely scored high on the other two. On the other hand, if you score low on one of the qualities, you likely scored low on the other two.
- It's common for scores to be the same for all three qualities.
- Most interestingly, the final number you got when you divided your total by 3 is likely the same number (or close to it) you gave yourself above when you rated how full your stress bucket is. This illustrates the point of this activity and one of the major points of

this workbook: *Your breathing reveals your stress!*

Feel Your Breathing, Feel Your Body

Feeling your breathing is a doorway into feeling your body. When you feel your breathing, you feel your body. An awareness of your body, specifically the presence or absence of tension in your body, informs you about your stress bucket levels. Stress manifests as tension in your body. Consequently, if you don't notice tension increasing in the body, then it just tightens and tightens until it consumes your attention and you can't ignore it anymore.

Let's briefly return to the water-in-the-bucket analogy. Imagine holding a bucket that's filling up with water. You pay no attention to the bucket until it "suddenly" feels heavy and, in the next moment, it's overfilling. Even though it might seem like the bucket suddenly overfilled, it didn't—it gradually filled up. It's just that while it was filling up, you weren't paying attention. In a similar way, if you don't pay attention to the stress filling up in your body, it will eventually overflow, and that's not good for you or anyone else.

Meet Jennifer, a junior in high school, who gets very anxious during math tests (or any test for that matter). When Jennifer initially walks into math class, her stress bucket is at a 4 or 5, but five minutes later, when she's three problems into her fifty-problem math test, her stress bucket suddenly floods to a 10.

We ask Jennifer what typically happens in those five minutes between walking into class and starting the test, and she has no idea. All she knows is that her bucket goes from an *I-feel-fine* "5" to an *I-feel-like-I'm-gonna-freak-out* "10."

Luckily for Jennifer, we're her friends, and we want to help her out because that's what good friends do. But how do we help her? Well, for starters, we invite her to pay attention to what her breathing and her body communicate between the time she walks into class and the beginning of her next math test. When Jennifer tries this out, she notices that in those few minutes between entering class and starting the test, her body communicated a lot of valuable information.

First, Jennifer notices that her stomach muscles tighten. Shortly after that, she clenches her jaw. The force of her clenched jaw creates tension down her neck into her shoulders—which changes her posture: her shoulders roll forward and her upper body slowly leans forward. The tightness in her stomach pulls her shoulders forward and down toward her hips.

Now because her posture is in a more collapsed position, her breathing becomes shallow. And because her breathing is more shallow, it speeds up, which causes her to breathe through her mouth. This makes her lose a lot of CO_2, which kicks off some emotional reactivity in her brain. The rising sense of panic causes her adrenal glands to pour some adrenaline into her blood stream, which speeds up her heart rate and causes a wave of warmth to flush over her body and face.

At this point, thoughts rush through Jennifer's mind, a surge of emotion floods her body, and the walls seem to close in on her—because her eyes have dilated and are taking in more information. Her body is sounding a threat alarm that ultimately makes her just want to sprint out of the classroom.

Jennifer's body provided a lot of important information. Notice how, back when she didn't pay attention, her anxiety came on "suddenly." But now she knows that what felt sudden to her wasn't actually sudden at all—it was the end result of her stress levels going unnoticed until they finally "overfilled her bucket" and grabbed her attention.

This is an important point: physical sensations of stress are messages your physiology sends to you in real time so that you can act on them and redirect your emotional state. When you don't pay attention to these messages, they get sent with greater urgency and strength (stronger sensations) until you pay attention. The problem, as Jennifer can attest to, is that if you ignore them for too long, they'll overrun your body and mind before you even know what's happening.

Your practice (and Jennifer's), then, is to become more aware of the process of stress and tension filling up in your body. Once you develop a deeper awareness of tension in your body, you'll have a better chance of interrupting and redirecting your stress by learning to empty the bucket with the "good" habits you identified in the last activity!

But first, to become more aware of what your body is telling you in real time, try the following practice:

Step 1: Find somewhere you can be still and quiet and pay attention to your body.

Step 2: Take a couple of minutes and get settled in a comfortable position. Lie down if you want or simply sit up straight.

Step 3: Give your current stress bucket a score again (1–10). Write it here:

Step 4: Once you've given your stress level a score, ask yourself: *Where in my body do I feel this score and what sensations do I feel?* For example, if you gave your stress level a 7, then maybe you feel the tightness in your shoulders. Whatever your score is, list the specific sensations and their location on the body image below. Identify as many sensations as possible.

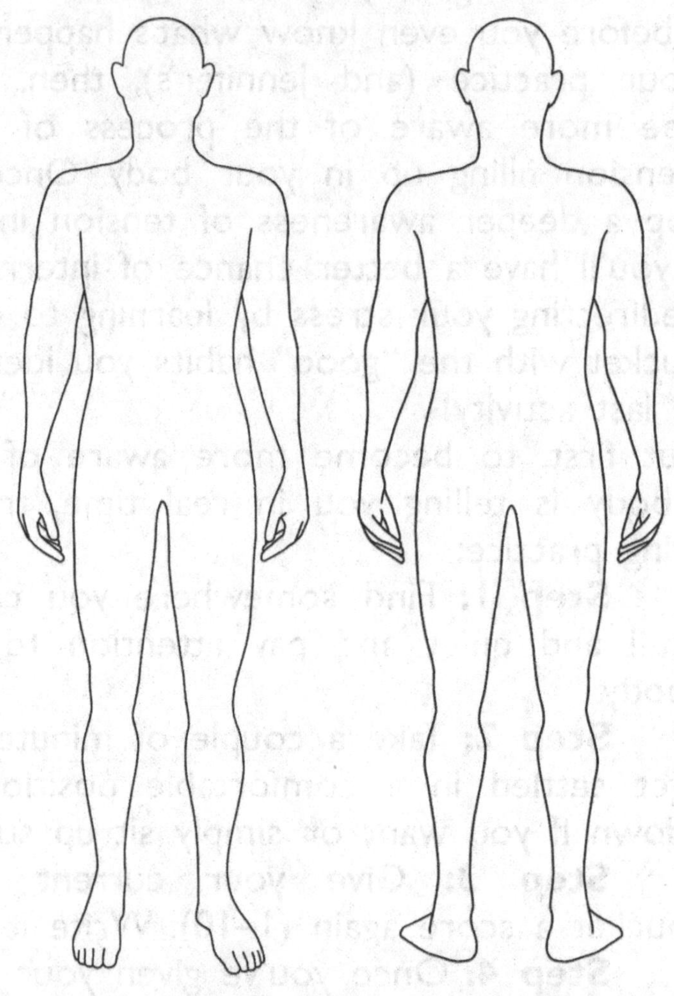

Now, based on what you identified on the image of a body, fill out this chart. In the first column, list the most noticeable sensations first and then move to the least noticeable sensations. In the second column, describe the quality of each sensation. I'll start with some examples for you.

Area of the Body (in order of most vividly felt)	Description of Sensation
1. My shoulders	• Tight with a dull ache
2. My jaw	• Tight and stiff
3. My neck	• Tight and stiff
4.	•
5.	•
6.	•
7.	•
8.	•
9.	•
10.	•

• Well done. Now, let's revisit Jennifer's story to see how an awareness of tension in her breathing and her body can empower her to more skillfully manage and redirect stressful emotions. Now that Jennifer is aware of the valuable information her body provides in real time, she can make adjustments and prevent her bucket from filling up to a 10. Here's what she does:

• When she notices her stomach and jaw tightening, she consciously relaxes them.

• When she notices her posture hunching forward, she sits up straight.

• When her breathing speeds up, she closes her mouth and slowly breathes through her nose.

When Jennifer takes conscious control of her body position and breathing like this, she tells the emotional centers of her brain that the situation is under control. Doing that keeps adrenaline out of her bloodstream and her heart rate normal—which prevents her from feeling warm and flushed. Finally, because she is consciously managing her physiology, her thoughts don't become volatile and reactive and she not only survives her math test, she crushes it!

Now it's your turn. Jennifer showed us how to skillfully manage stressful bodily sensations with mindful awareness. Fill in the first column the same way you did in the previous table, and then, in the second column, identify mindful adjustments that you can make. I'll start you off with a couple of examples.

Area of the Body (in order of most vividly felt)	Mindful Adjustments That I Can Make
1. My shoulders	• Roll them around and raise them toward my ears and then relax them.
2. My neck	• Release any tension in my jaw and gently stretch my neck by rocking my head side-to-side, forward and backward.
3.	•
4.	•
5.	•
6.	•
7.	•
8.	•
9.	•
10.	•

Well done, my friend. The more you practice these adjustments, the easier they'll be to make when you need to make them. Remember: When you feel "stressed," pay attention to your breathing and your body. Identify where there is tension, and then make the necessary adjustments.

BIG Idea: In your own words, what's one BIG idea that will stick with you from this activity? In other words, what's an idea that you connected with or that made you think in a new way? Why was it impactful?

____

____

____

____

Essential Takeaway: Sometimes the feeling of stress seems hard to pinpoint. But if you mindfully attend to your breathing and your body, you see that stress always arises as tension in your breathing and your body. Like a stress thermostat, your breathing and your body tell you if your stress levels are too high or too low. When you can pinpoint the source of tension, you can then consciously employ skillful stress-management habits and restore calm.

9

record your stress levels over time

Let's now look at some trends that repeatedly cause your stress bucket to fill—and overfill. What are the specific conditions (like skipping sleep or fixating too much on schoolwork) in your life that cause stress and anxiety? Understanding the conditions that influence your stress levels empowers you to create more ideal conditions that allow you to live and perform at your best—while avoiding the conditions that weaken your emotional well-being.

What conditions am I talking about? Well, a good place to start is with HALT (hungry, angry, lonely, and tired) states. HALT states are conditions and triggers for stress and poor decision making. Let's identify how these HALT conditions—and any others you can think of, like sadness—show up in your life. Identifying and understanding these patterns allows you to make skillful changes to soothe your stress and boost your emotional well-being.

We'll start with a broad view of your stress levels over the last year and then eventually narrow it down to the last twenty-four hours.

Then we'll explore the conditions (think HALT to start—if you need to) that influence your stress levels.

The Past Year

Can you map out the general fluctuations in your stress levels (1–10) over the course of the past year? For example, here's my last year:

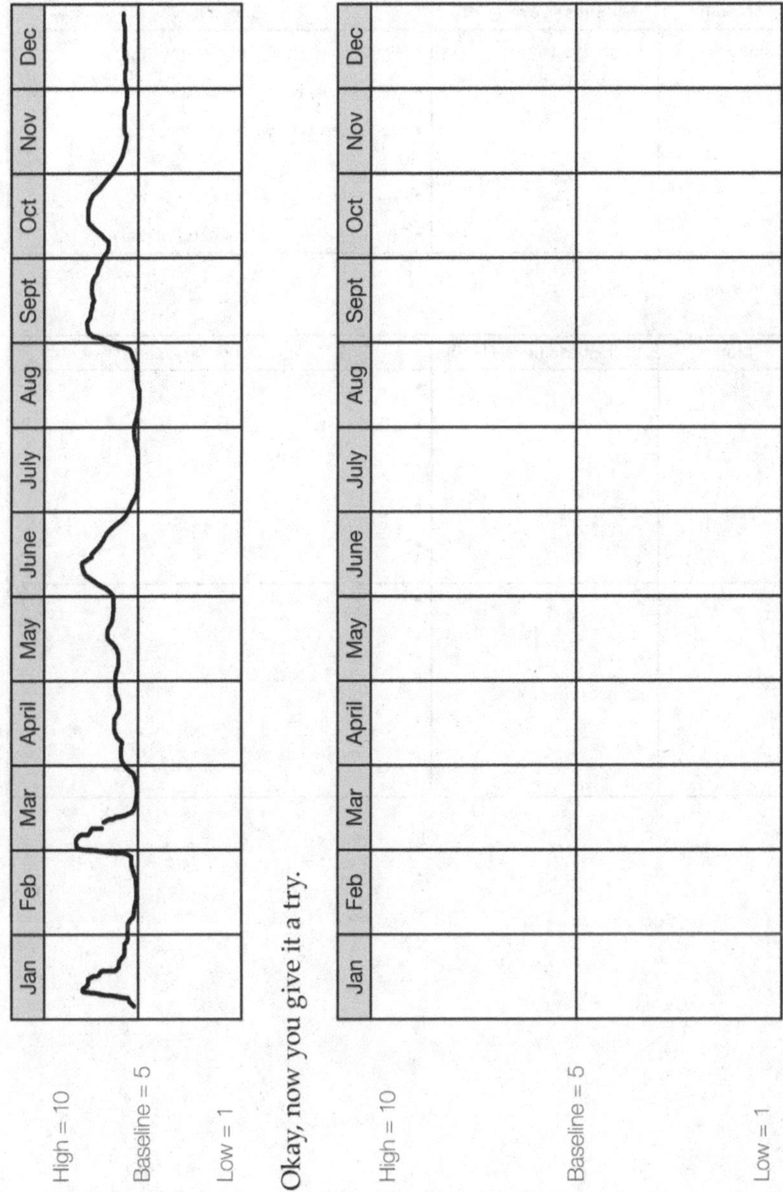

Okay, now you give it a try.

Now recall and explain the factors behind the ebbs and flows of your stress levels over the past year. I've shared mine for January. I'll get you started with my own example.

Month:	My Stress Level (1–10)	Conditions
January	My stress was frequently about a 7-8	• My godmother passed away • Got a really bad case of the flu • Scheduled way too many presentations in a row • Had a lot of grading to do • The weather was cold and dreary

Month:	Your Stress Level (1–10)	Conditions
January		• • • • •
February		• • • • •

Month:	Your Stress Level (1–10)	Conditions
March		• • • • •
April		• • • • •
May		• • • • •
June		• • • • •

Month:	Your Stress Level (1–10)	Conditions
July		• • • • •
August		• • • • •
September		• • • • •
October		• • • • •

Month:	Your Stress Level (1–10)	Conditions
November		• • • • •
December		• • • • •

What kind of year did you have overall? Identify any recurring connections between your stress levels and their surrounding conditions. Write down any observations or insights about your stress levels and patterns over the past year.

The Past Month

Can you map out the general fluctuations in your stress levels over the last 30 days?

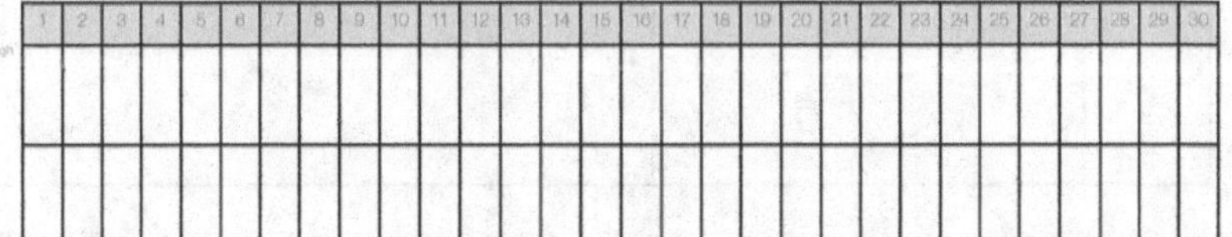

Great! Now recall and explain the conditions surrounding the ebbs and flows of your stress levels over the past month, grouping them into weeks.

Week	Your Stress Level (1–10)	Conditions
1		• • • • •
2		• • • • •

Week	Your Stress Level (1–10)	Conditions
3		• • • • •
4		• • • • •

As you did before, identify any recurring connections between your stress levels and their surrounding conditions. Write down any observations or insights about your stress levels and patterns over the past month.

The Past Week

Map out the general fluctuations in your stress levels over the course of the last week.

	Day 1	Day 2	Day 3	Day 4	Day 5	Day 6	Day 7
High = 10							
Baseline = 5							
Low = 1							

Now identify the factors influencing the ebbs and flows of your stress levels over the past seven days.

Day	Your Stress Level (1–10)	Conditions
1		• • • • •

Day	Your Stress Level (1–10)	Conditions
2		• • • • •
3		• • • • •
4		• • • • •
5		• • • • •

Day	Your Stress Level (1–10)	Conditions
6		• • • • •
7		• • • • •

How did this week go? Identify any recurring connections between your stress levels and their surrounding conditions. Write down any observations or insights about your stress levels and patterns over the past week.

The Past Twenty-Four Hours

Okay, last one. Fill in the blank hour boxes on the top and then map out the ebbs and flows of your stress levels over the past twenty-four hours.

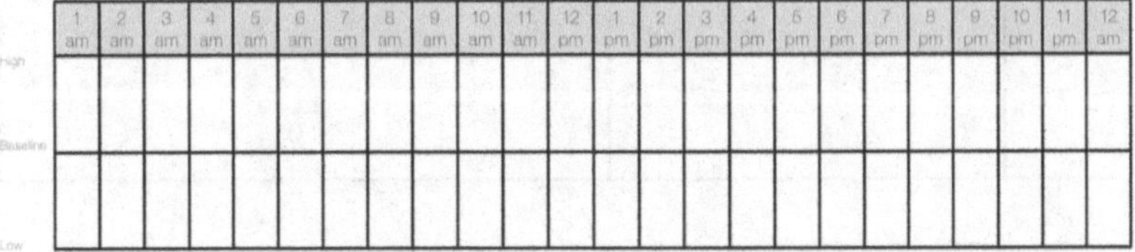

Now identify the factors influencing the ebbs and flows of your stress levels over the past twenty-four hours, grouping them into morning, afternoon, evening, and night.

	Your Stress Level (1–10)	Conditions
Morning		• • • • •
Afternoon		• • • • •

	Your Stress Level (1–10)	Conditions
Evening		• • • • •
Night		• • • • •

How has your day been? Identify any recurring connections between your stress levels and their surrounding conditions. Write down any observations or insights about your stress levels and patterns over the past day.

Overview of Your Stress-Level Mapping

Okay, take a step back and look at the stress-level mapping you've done for the past year, month, week, and day. Identify three conditions that consistently influence your stress levels across the different time frames. List them here in order of significance:

1. ____________________
2. ____________________
3. ____________________

Can you describe specifically how each of these circumstances impacts your stress levels? I'll jump in here and share my own example first:

My Condition 1: When I look at my stress levels across the different time frames, I see a recurring connection between overcommitting myself to work and my stress levels. Over and over again, I see my stress spiking during times of the year, month, week, and day when I'm attempting to do too many things at once, and

I'm not giving myself enough to time to step back, rest, and recover.

Okay, now it's your turn. For each condition you listed above, describe how it impacts your stress levels.

Condition 1: ______________

____

____

Condition 2: ______________

____

____

Condition 3: ______________

____

____

Now describe why you ranked them in this order. In other words, what makes condition 1 more influential on your stress than conditions 2 and 3?

____

____

____

____

____

To end this activity, ponder some practical life adjustments you can make to change or offset the conditions that most negatively influence your stress. I'll give you a personal example:

My Life Adjustment Example: I need to practice saying no. Because I have a zest for life and love working with people and taking on new and challenging projects, I tend to say yes to too many things. This leaves me over committed and under rested, which ultimately fills my stress bucket up and keeps those stress levels too high for too long. By saying no more, I can reduce the amount of hoses filling my bucket and enjoy the things that I do commit to.

Now, your turn! Describe the three life adjustments you can make to lessen the impact of the stress-inducing conditions you identified.

Life Adjustment 1: __________

____

____

____

____

Life Adjustment 2: __________

____

____

____

____

Life Adjustment 3: __________

____

____

____

____

That was a lot, but you did it. Be proud of yourself! Now you have some insight into your stress levels over time, the conditions that cause them, and the real-time adjustments you can make to restore balance in your life.

BIG Idea: In your own words, what's one BIG idea that will stick with you from this activity? In other words, what's an idea that you connected with or that made you think in a new way? Why was it impactful?

____

____

____

____

Essential Takeaway: Looking at our stress levels over time isn't something most of us are inclined to do on our own, but stick to it! Just because you did it once doesn't mean you never have to do it again. The real value of this activity lies in doing it continually: periodically make it a point to step back and revisit trends in your stress, its precipitating conditions, and the adjustments you can make to destress and live well.

Section Two Reflection

That's a wrap. Section two is in the books. Nice effort. You've learned a lot. So take a moment to bring it all together. I'll get you started:

- Pay attention to changes in your breathing, which are the first sign of stress. Your breathing changes in real time to help your physiology adjust to increasing levels of stress. Also pay attention to what your physiology tells you through the quality of your breathing (weight, rate, and depth) and your CO_2 tolerance.
- Be mindful of how full your stress bucket is and attempt to lower it using good stress-management strategies. Remember: your worst habits are unskillful attempts to manage your stress.
- Pay attention to what your breathing and your body tell you about your stress levels.
- Record your stress levels over time and identify the conditions that influence them.

Describe what was most impactful from section two.

____

____

How might this change what you do moving forward?

____

____

SECTION THREE

Improve Your Breathing to Improve Your Emotional Control

Because you probably haven't thought much about your breathing for most of your life, you likely have developed some unskillful breathing habits. Consequently, it's worth our time to revisit the basics of mindful breathing: posture, mechanics, and tempo. Revisiting, improving, and practicing the *how to* of breathing will ensure that you get the results you're looking for—like better stress management and emotional control—from your mindful breathing practice.

10

sit up straight

You might think that you know how to breathe because you're breathing all of the time. To some extent, you're right: in the most basic sense, your innate breathing instincts keep you alive. But there's a big difference between breathing to merely survive and mindfully breathing to thrive. Mindful breathing is about using your breathing to manage your emotions and become your best self—and you can't achieve this without a mindful breathing practice!

So how do you turn unconscious breathing into a conscious skill? By breaking down, paying attention to, and practicing the different aspects of mindful breathing so that you can learn to better identify your emotions, shift out of bad moods, and find ease.

Posture Is a Big Deal

Every day I witness the impact of excessive technology use on students' posture. As I walk through the school, I often see students sitting, slouched forward, staring at their phones or computers. More and more, the typical young adult posture is starting to resemble the letter *C*.

When students stand up to walk to class, they're stuck in this posture that puts them into a permanent forward fold with rounded backs, forward shoulders, and a "goose neck" that sticks the head and ears out in front of their shoulders and body.

Poor posture from hours upon hours spent hunched over your computer or phone, combined with the normal emotional stress that comes with being a young adult, can create tense, restricted, and shallow breathing patterns. These dysregulated breathing patterns make your normal emotional stress levels worse by not allowing your physiology to efficiently regulate that stress through efficient breathing—which is your physiology's first line of defense against stress.

So yes, your posture is *very* important. Without good posture, there is no good breathing—and without good breathing, there are no good emotional or physical health outcomes. Now, notice what a good posture looks like: a straight line with the shoulders over the hips and the ears over the shoulders.

Poor Posture

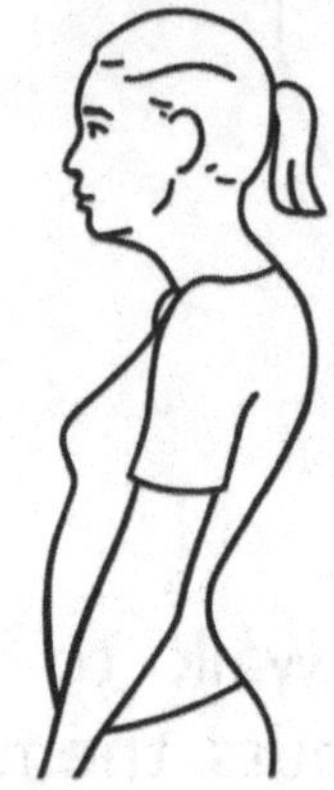

Good Posture

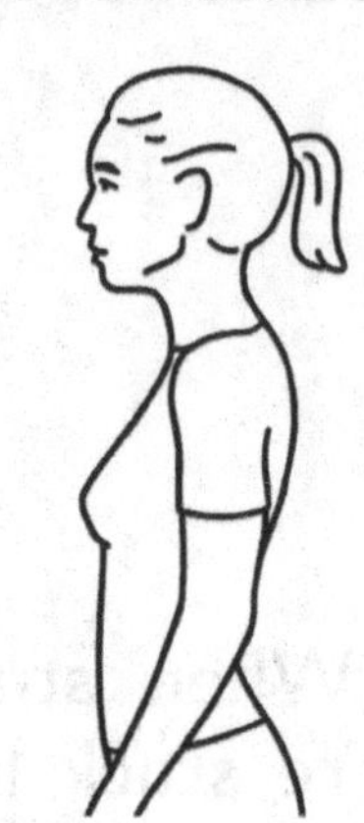

You might wonder: what makes the alignment of your hips, ears, and shoulders a "good" posture? First, it places your muscles in the correct position, which prevents unnecessary strain and fatigue by allowing them to work efficiently. Second, a vertically organized spine heightens attention. This just means that when you sit or stand up straight, you're sending a message to your brain to be alert and "pay attention." Last, and most importantly, in terms of mindful breathing, when you sit and stand up straight, you give your ribcage space to fully expand and contract, which gives your diaphragm muscle enough space to efficiently initiate the breathing process.

We'll talk more about the diaphragm in an upcoming activity, but for now, let me just say that it's the largest and most important muscle for your breathing. It's an umbrella-shaped muscle that spans across your whole torso. When you inhale, it flattens, and when you exhale, it turns into a dome to push the air out. Most importantly, in relation to your posture, when you sit or stand hunched forward, your ribs get pinned down and your diaphragm cannot efficiently move air into and out of your body.

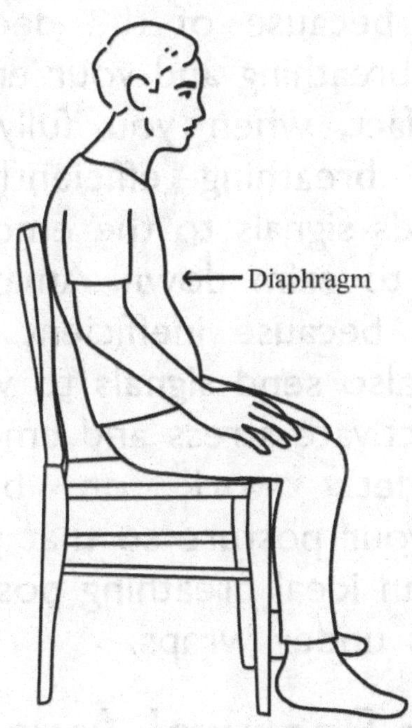

Consequently, the diaphragm has to work harder to get air in and out of the body—which means you're going to breathe more and get less out of each breath. This breathing pattern is inefficient, ultimately leads to dysregulated breathing patterns, and eventually can lead to dysregulated emotional patterns because you have to breathe more shallowly—which often leads to excessive mouth breathing. And, as you remember from the last section, that's where the wheels start to fall off the bus!

Furthermore, there's a very important nerve that runs from your diaphragm to your brain called the phrenic nerve. The word "phrenic" actually comes from the Greek word *phren,* which means "mind." The phrenic nerve is called the "mind nerve" because of the deep connection between your breathing and your emotional state, or mind. In fact, when you fully activate the diaphragm by breathing efficiently with good posture, it sends signals to the emotional centers of your brain to calm down. Amazing, right? Be careful though because inefficient breathing and poor posture also send signals to your brain, but these signals activate stress and emotional unrest. Okay, now let's work on building more awareness of your posture so that you can spend more time in an ideal breathing posture and keep your emotions under wraps.

Build Your Postural Awareness

Here's what you need to do to make sure that your posture allows you to access your diaphragm, breathe efficiently, and keep your emotions on track:

Step 1: Stand up and get into your normal posture (make no special effort to stand "correctly"). Simply stand how you always normally stand.

Step 2: Give someone your phone and ask them to take a picture of you from the side. Or, if no one is around, you can try to stand in front of the mirror and look at yourself from the side. The problem with looking in the mirror is that you'll have to turn your head to look at yourself, and you'll also be more likely to adjust your posture as you look at yourself. In either case, you'll have the ability to see your default posture.

Step 3: Once you've seen your default posture, then get into an ideal posture (shoulders over hips, ears over shoulders). Again, have someone take your picture or a video, or look in a mirror. As you assume an ideal posture, pay attention to the adjustments that you need to make to get there: Maybe your neck is too far forward and you have to gently bring your chin in and back. Maybe your shoulders are rolled forward and you have to set them back. Maybe your ribs and chest are also collapsed forward, and you have to gently elevate your chest. You get the idea. Pay attention to the adjustments you make.

Step 4: Once you've established an ideal posture, hold it for a few minutes.

Feel free to walk around or stand right where you are, but whatever you decide to do, pay attention to how it feels to be in that posture and if it feels any different in terms of the quality of your breathing.

When you looked at a picture or video of your default posture (or observed yourself in the mirror), what did you notice? What did your default posture look like? Remember, start by identifying if your shoulders were over your hips and your ears were over your shoulders. Write down what you saw.

____

____

____

____

What corrections did you have to make to your posture? Be specific. For example, did you move your shoulders back to be over your hips or your ears back to be over your shoulders?

____

____

____

____

How did it feel once you established a more aligned posture? Was it more comfortable? Less comfortable? Were you able to breathe more effortlessly? No difference? Write down some general observations about what you felt.

How did your breathing feel? Light? Heavy? Relaxed? Tense? Write some specific observations.

For one week, document the activities and times of day when you're most likely to find yourself in a compromised posture. Then make a note on what aspect of your posture was out of alignment.

Day	Activity/Time	Postural Details
Sunday	• • •	• • •
Monday	• • •	• • •
Tuesday	• • •	• • •

Day	Activity/Time	Postural Details
Wednesday	• • •	• • •
Thursday	• • •	• • •
Friday	• • •	• • •
Saturday	• • •	• • •

Looking back on your week, what do you notice? Was there an activity that consistently compromised your posture?

____

____

Was there a time of day when you were more likely to be in a compromised posture? Explain.

____

____

Was there a particular position that you repeatedly defaulted to?

Paying attention to and continually correcting your posture is no small task. It's so easy to default to the poor postural habits we've become accustomed to in our society. But if you're going to get the most out of your mindful breathing practice, then you have to position yourself in a manner that allows your diaphragm the space to do its work!

Perform Daily Postural Exercises

Consider incorporating basic postural exercises and stretches into your day-to-day life to support and restore an ideal posture and optimal breathing patterns. These exercises will address your posture from the bottom up. This approach is important because if you perform exercises to correct forward head posture, for example, you won't get very far if your thoracic spine (mid-back) remains tight and rounded forward. Consequently, we're going to address and retrain your posture from the bottom up.

As you do these exercises, pay close attention to your breathing. If you're holding your breath, you're likely being too forceful with your movements. Your breathing constricts when your nervous system senses the stress of excessive muscular strain. So ease up and listen to your breath. Only stretch to the extent that you can breathe comfortably. You should feel no strain or pain—just a nice and easy stretch.

I selected these exercises based on their simplicity, effectiveness, and convenience. There are many, many more restorative postural exercises that you can do. If you have the ability to do so, schedule an appointment with a physical therapist or a qualified personal trainer who specializes in functional exercise and postural mechanics. Before doing these exercises, especially if you have any physical limitations or conditions, check with your doctor to make sure these are safe for you.

Strengthen Your Core with the Plank

Core strength is essential for proper posture because it positions and holds your torso in place so that you can breathe properly. When your core is weak, many other muscles have to compensate (like your hip flexors), which will cause tightness and poor breathing mechanics in the long run. The "plank" is a basic exercise you can perform daily to strengthen your core. It looks like this:

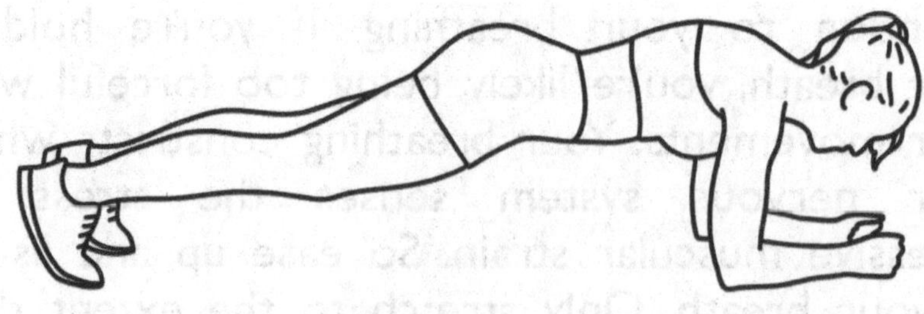

Step 1: Get down on your hands and knees and then place your elbows directly beneath your shoulders on the ground. Put the bottom of your toes on the ground, lift your knees, and slide your elbows forward until your body is in a straight line. Feel free to tighten your hands into fists (as shown) or keep your forearms and hands pointed directly forward.

Step 2: Maintain a straight body line from head to heels. Do not lift your butt up or let it sag down, as shown in the next two illustrations.

Step 3: Squeeze your butt and flex your abs as if someone is going to punch you in the gut!

Step 4: Imagine trying to pull the ground down with your arms and up with your feet.

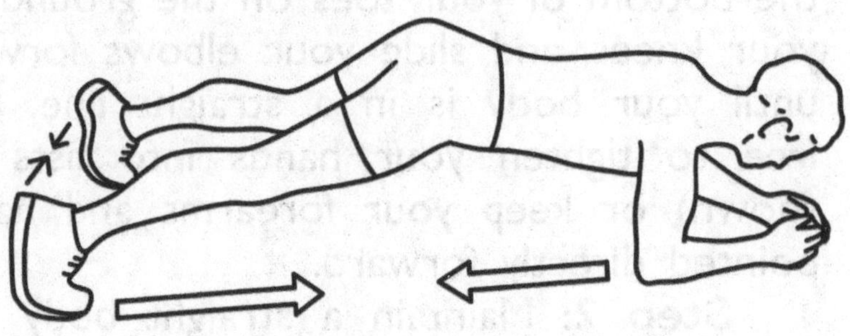

Step 5: Pay attention to your breathing. As you engage your abs, your breathing will tend to constrict, but do your best to continue to breathe normally. Keep your mouth closed and breathe through your nose.

Step 6: Hold for as long as you can and keep working to improve your time. The current world record is only 8 hours, 15 minutes, and 15 seconds. You can do it! (wink, wink)

Go ahead and give it a try, and record your plank time right here:

Unlock Your Thoracic Spine with Cat/Cow Pose

When you constantly sit in a forward-leaning position, the muscles that support the movement of your thoracic spine get very tight. This causes the movement and flexibility of your spine to be reduced, leaving your spine "stuck" in a position that keeps your upper body in improper position and alignment.

The thoracic spine is also very important to your breathing because it's where all of your ribs connect to your spine. So if your thoracic spine is really tight, then your ribs are going to be less able to expand and contract as you breathe. By opening up your thoracic spine, you also free up your ribs and ultimately allow your diaphragm to work efficiently.

Step 1: Position yourself on your hands and knees and place your hands below your shoulders with your knees below your hips. Feel your breathing and relax.

Step 2: Slowly inhale and curl your toes under. Tilt your pelvis back so that your tailbone sticks up, and gently arch your back, vertebrae by vertebrae, from your tailbone all the way up into your neck. Your belly will sink, but keep your abdominal muscles hugging your spine by drawing your bellybutton in. Slowly and gently raise your gaze up toward the ceiling without straining your neck. Once you feel your whole torso and neck fully extend, pause and enjoy the stretch.

Step 3: Now, slowly exhale and let the tops of your feet fall to the floor. Tip your pelvis forward, tucking in your tailbone. Let this tuck ripple up your spine from your tailbone through your neck, creating a rounded spine. Draw your navel toward your spine and then gently release and drop your head toward the floor, shifting your gaze to your navel.

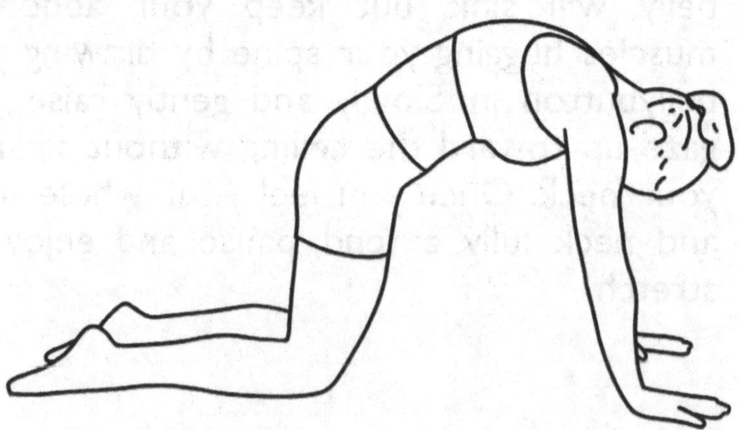

Step 4: Following the flow of your breath, gently and mindfully transition back and forth between steps 2 and 3 five to ten times. Finish on an exhale and with a neutral spine.

Free Your Ribcage with the Side-Bend Stretch

Step 1: Stand straight and tall with feet and legs apart.

Step 2: Reach both arms straight up overhead and, if you can, clasp your hands as you inhale.

Step 3: Gently engage your abdominal muscles, slowly lower your right arm down the right side of your body, and exhale as you lengthen and reach your left arm over your head, bending your body gently to the right.

Step 4: Inhale as you return to the center position with arms overhead, and then exhale as you repeat step 3 on the left side.

Open Your Chest with the Door Frame Stretch

Step 1: Stand in an open doorway. Raise both arms up to the side, bent at 90-degree angles with palms forward.

Step 2: Rest your palms on the door frame and pinch your shoulder blades together before you start stretching. This ensures that your shoulder joint is protected. If you don't do this, you risk stretching tendons instead of muscles.

Step 3: Slowly step forward with one foot until you feel a stretch in the front of your shoulders and chest. Do not be forceful with the stretch. Ease into it because, again, your shoulder is in a vulnerable position. And make sure you feel stretching in your muscles and not in your joint. Keep your abdominal muscles tight and do not overextend your lower back during the stretch. Stop the stretch immediately if you have any tingling sensations in your fingers, hands, or arms.

Step 4: Hold for 10 to 15 seconds; then gently ease out of the stretch and step back. Let your arms come down and shake them out for 10 to 15 seconds. Repeat three times.

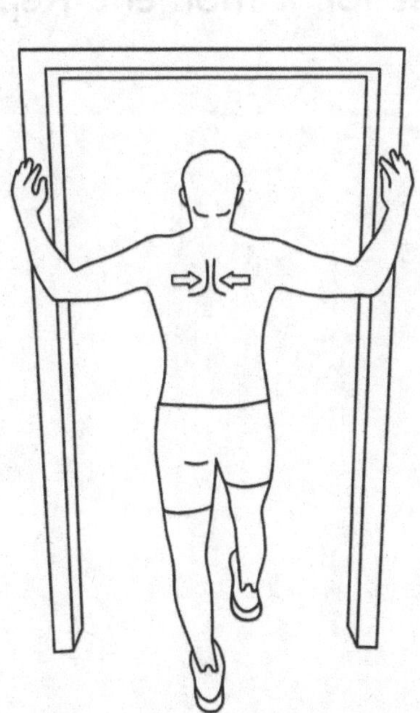

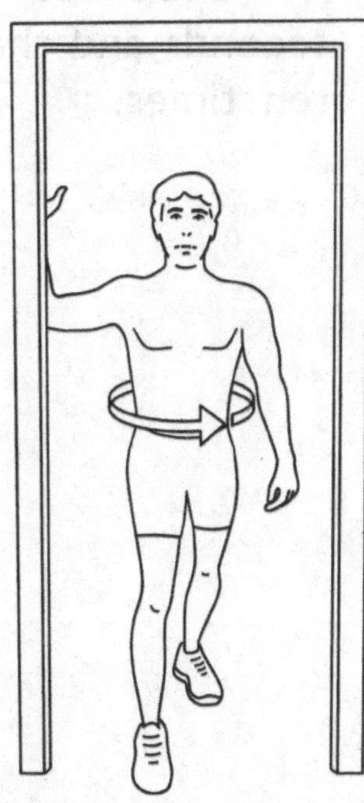

Variation: For a gentler or different version of this exercise, try the one-armed version. Follow the same steps but with only one hand on the door frame. Turn your torso as the arrow in the illustration above shows.

Correct Your Neck Position with the Chin Tuck

Step 1: Stand with your back against the wall, feet shoulder-width apart, heels an inch or so from the wall.

Step 2: Facing forward, tuck your chin down and pull your head back until it touches the wall.

Step 3: Hold that position for 5 seconds and then rest for a moment. Repeat ten times.

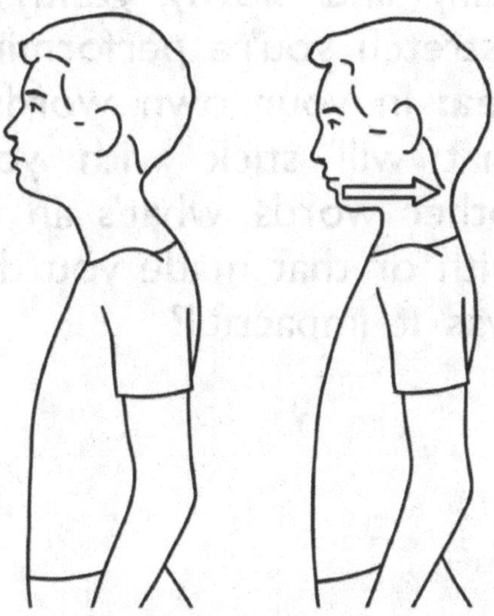

What did you notice while doing these exercises? Were they difficult? Easy? Did you discover an area of your body that is weak and/or tight? Describe your experience with these exercises.

Stretching, especially when you're not accustomed to it, can cause feelings of agitation, frustration, and stress. Bringing awareness to tight muscles also brings awareness to "tight" thoughts and feelings. If and when you notice these thoughts and feelings arise, observe them nonjudgmentally and slowly, gently ease up on the specific stretch you're performing.

BIG Idea: In your own words, what's one BIG idea that will stick with you from this activity? In other words, what's an idea that you connected with or that made you think in a new way? Why was it impactful?

____

____

____

____

Essential Takeaway: Mindful breathing begins with an awareness of your posture so that you can maintain the optimal position to breathe most effectively and efficiently. Our societal norms, primarily involving technology, have led to widespread problems with posture. Because poor posture interferes with optimal breathing, I encourage you to make stretching and postural exercises a regular part of your mindful breathing practice.

11

choose your formal breathing posture

As you start to develop a mindful breathing practice, it's helpful to explore "formal" breathing postures. Each of the three postures you'll practice in this activity keeps the torso upright, with the shoulders over the hips and the ears over the shoulders, allowing you to practice mindful breathing most effectively. Again, this creates a sense of clarity and calm because you have full access to your diaphragm muscle, which can then do its job efficiently.

Experiment with each of these three formal sitting postures and then identify which one works the best for you. Try each posture out for a few minutes and record what you felt and experienced.

Cross-Legged Posture

Describe what sitting in this posture felt like.
My breathing felt...

My body felt...

My attention felt...

Kneeling Posture

Describe what sitting in this posture felt like.
My breathing felt...

My body felt...

My attention felt...

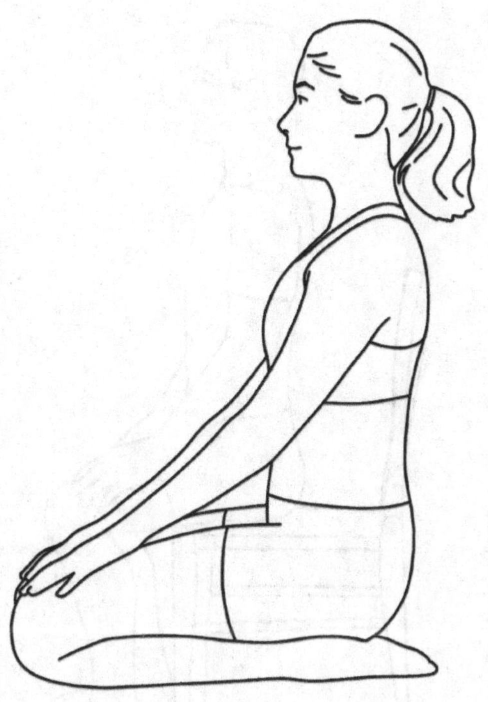

Chair Posture

Describe what sitting in this posture felt like.
My breathing felt...

My body felt...

My attention felt...

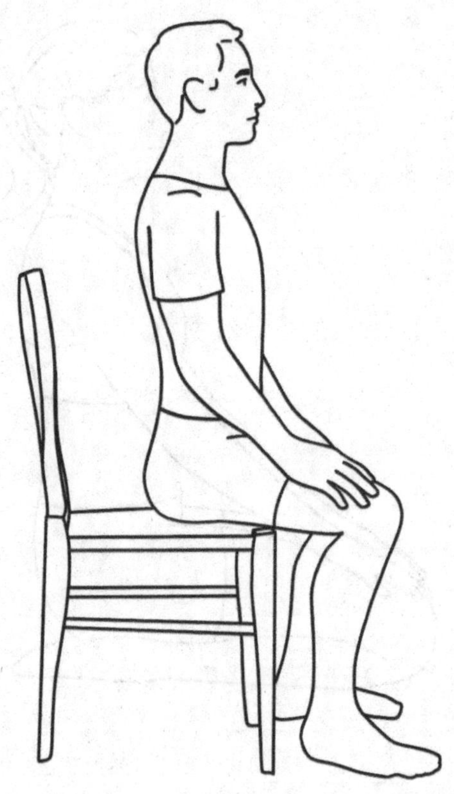

Now that you've experienced all three postures, which one is the most comfortable overall for you to do your breathing practice? Explain why.

Give yourself time and experience to find the ideal posture for your mindful breathing practice. Be sure to experiment with all three postures before settling on one.

BIG Idea: In your own words, what's one BIG idea that will stick with you from this activity? In other words, what's an idea that you connected with or that made you think in a new way? Why was it impactful?

Essential Takeaway: Maintaining a straight vertical line through the hips, shoulders, and ears ensures that your breathing mechanics will be on point. There are three formal breathing postures that achieve this ideal alignment. Again, practice them all before settling on one.

12

shut your mouth! (and breathe through your nose)

One of the most important suggestions offered in this workbook is to develop the habit of breathing through your nose, especially while you sleep. You are meant to breathe through your nose, with the only exceptions being when you eat, talk, and engage in maximum-effort exercise. So, if you only remember one thing from this workbook, remember to breathe through your nose! Seriously.

As I discussed earlier, when you're chronically stressed out, you can develop the habit of overbreathing. One of the consequences of overbreathing is that you start to breathe through your mouth, which results in offloading too much CO_2. Well, you can stop this vicious cycle by breathing through your nose.

Breathing through your nose lessens and regulates the amount of CO_2 you can exhale. Go ahead and see for yourself: Put the back of a finger or two under your nose and feel a normal exhalation. Then open your mouth, put the back of your hand in front of your mouth, and feel a normal exhalation through your mouth. Big difference, right?!

With more CO_2 in your system, your physiology becomes more efficient with oxygen (this is actually known as the "Bohr effect"—ask your science teacher about it!), and with greater aerobic (oxygen) efficiency, your whole physiology, including your emotions, will be more regulated.

Pay Attention to Mouth Breathing

For twenty-four hours, pay attention to how often you breathe through your mouth. And I want you to list what you were doing (outside of talking, eating, and intense exercise) when you caught yourself breathing through your mouth. Pay particular attention to whether you breathe through your mouth while you're sleeping. How do you do this if you are asleep? Well, by noticing a few things when you wake up, like ... were you drooling (yup, I'm for real)? Was your mouth really dry? Did someone mention that you were snoring?

Beyond sleeping, also pay attention to mouth breathing throughout the day. When you notice that you are, just simply make a note, close your mouth, and return to breathing through your nose. When you're done with your twenty-four-hour field study, write what you discovered below.

Mouth-Breathing Field Notes

I noticed I unconsciously breathe through my mouth when I'm...

____

____

____

____

____

____

____

____

Good work. Now, if you find that you're a chronic mouth breather, what should you do?

Identify if your mouth breathing is caused my something physical, like a deviated septum, seasonal allergies, a cold, or the flu. If you can't physically breathe through your nose, you obviously have to breathe through your mouth until your nose and sinuses are cleared. Talk to a doctor if you consistently have difficulty breathing through your nose.

In the absence of any physical explanation, your mouth breathing is likely an unconscious and unskillful strategy to mitigate stress. Like many other unconscious and unskillful stress-management strategies, it only creates more stress in the long run. So, if you recognize an emotional stress pattern underlying your mouth breathing, check your CO_2 tolerance using the assessment in section two, activity 6. If you discover that it is low, improving your CO_2 tolerance using the exercises below will help reverse the instinct to mouth breathe.

Exercises to Shift Your Default to Nasal Breathing

Here are some exercises you can do to train yourself to shift from mouth breathing to nose breathing. (If you have panic disorder, high blood pressure, and/or asthma, talk to a physician before doing these exercises, and do them cautiously.)

Exercise #1: Breathing through your nose, slow your breathing down so much that you create a mild sense of breathlessness. Tolerate it as best you can, and then restore normal breathing when you need to. Continue this pattern for as long as you want. Five minutes is a good place to start.

Exercise #2: Do moderate exercise—for example, a brisk walk, a jog, or a bike ride—and breathe only through your nose. If you reach a level of exertion where you feel like you need to breathe through your mouth, then dial back the intensity until you can breathe only through your nose again. If you're an athlete, throughout the next three weeks, do all of your training with nasal breathing only. At the end of the three weeks, you should notice that nasal breathing feels more natural and that your endurance has improved.

Exercise #3: Practice holding your breath *after you exhale.* If you have panic attacks or asthma, holding your breath can induce anxiety and breathlessness because of the underlying CO_2 intolerance. Talk to your doctor first and be very gentle with this exercise. Only do what is comfortable. Don't push it.

Here's how to do it: Typically, when you're going to hold your breath, you do it after a big inhale. Not this time. After a *normal exhale,* time how long you can hold your breath. This is very similar to the CO_2 assessment in section two—except now you're going to see how long you can actually hold your breath (rather than stopping at the first sign of air hunger). Time yourself and keep track of your scores so that you can see if there's improvement. If you do this exercise more than once at a time, be sure to give yourself a few minutes in between holds. Over time, this exercise will help improve your CO_2 tolerance and make it more comfortable for you to breathe through your nose—because, again, it's this underlying intolerance to CO_2 that often drives mouth breathing.

Exercise #4: Again, assuming you have no physical reason behind your mouth breathing or any other health condition (always consult your doctor first), experiment with taping your mouth with 3M Micropore Paper Tape before you go to sleep and keeping it on while sleeping. Yes, this sounds crazy, but it can be life changing (I know from personal experience). The tape comes off pretty painlessly but is strong enough to help keep your mouth closed. Watch videos online for how to apply the tape (you don't need a lot).

If this idea scares you (which it initially did for me), try taping your mouth for periods of time while you're awake. Once you get used to it, try taping your mouth for a nap. Eventually, you'll be able to give it a try for a whole night, and you'll see the results when you wake up. If you can swing it, this is a great exercise because it provides eight hours of free nasal breathing practice, and you don't even have to pay attention—because you're asleep!

I know these exercises aren't easy, but your willingness to do them is commendable. Good job!

BIG Idea: In your own words, what's one BIG idea that will stick with you from this activity? In other words, what's an idea that you connected with or that made you think in a new way? Why was it impactful?

____

____

____

____

Essential Takeaway: Close your mouth and breathe through your nose. Not only is mouth breathing inefficient, it can lead to chronic overbreathing, CO_2 intolerance, and emotional reactivity. Pay attention to whether you are breathing through your mouth or nose, and practice the exercises in this activity to train yourself to shift to nasal breathing.

13

breathe lightly, slowly, and deeply

Now that your posture is on point and you're effortlessly breathing through your nose, you're ready to focus your attention on how to breathe to manage your stress and anxiety. As I've mentioned numerous times throughout this workbook, your emotions and how you breathe are deeply connected. Now let's use your breathing to influence your emotions.

Because most of us don't pay attention to our posture or our breathing in general, it has become natural for many of us to breathe *heavily, rapidly,* and *shallowly*—all of which are signs of overbreathing (which is itself a symptom of emotional stress and compromised breathing mechanics). So, what's the solution, you ask? Simple: As Patrick McKeon, one of my breathing instructors, would say, breathe *lightly, slowly,* and *deeply.* But despite what most people think, deep breathing isn't something you consciously do—rather, it's what naturally happens when you're breathing correctly (lightly and slowly through your nose) with good posture. Often, when you're stressed out, you initiate a loud, forceful "deep" sigh to calm down. Unfortunately, this doesn't help, and it only perpetuates the chronic overbreathing patterns that make our stress and anxiety worse. The key to relaxing and breathing deeply is to breathe lightly and slowly!

The following breathing exercises are geared toward helping you breathe lightly, slowly, and deeply. I recommend this first one if you're experiencing mild to moderate stress.

Step 1: Get into your breathing posture of choice (see activity 11). Take a few minutes to anchor your attention on your breathing and your body and establish nasal breathing if you're breathing through your mouth (which you shouldn't be!).

Step 2: When you're ready, bring your attention to the sound of your own breathing. Usually, it's the sound of air passing in and out of your nostrils.

Step 3: Begin to breathe more lightly until the sound of air passing through your nostrils goes away.

Step 4: Now that you've quieted your breathing, slow it down so that you can barely feel your breath enter and exit your nostrils.

Step 5: At this point, if you're breathing lightly and slowly and you're maintaining postural alignment, your breathing will naturally deepen by itself.

Step 6: Give yourself 5 to 10 minutes of breathing lightly, slowly, and deeply to destress and bring yourself back into balance.

This next exercise is a little different. I recommend it if you're experiencing moderate to severe stress and anxiety. I know from personal experience that it absolutely takes the edge off of stress and anxiety.

Step 1: Get into your breathing posture of choice and establish nasal breathing if you're breathing through your mouth. Take a few minutes to anchor your attention on your breathing and your body.

Step 2: When you're ready, draw in a long, slow breath and fill your lungs up to about 75% capacity—then pause for 1 to 2 seconds.

Step 3: Continue breathing in slowly the rest of the way until your lungs are 100% full (don't be forceful).

Step 4: This is important: Slowly exhale through the mouth like you're blowing on a hot cup of tea to cool it off. Ideally, the length of your exhalation should be longer than the length of your inhalation (up to twice as long). If you inhaled for 4 seconds, then try to exhale for 8 seconds. This will require that you slow your exhalation down.

Step 5: Repeat this breathing pattern for 5 minutes.

The best way to get good at these techniques is to practice them every day so that when you do find yourself in the throes of stress, you can immediately and skillfully implement them and redirect your state back to calm. Just remember the next time you find your stress bucket levels rising, breathe *lightly, slowly,* and *deeply!*

BIG Idea: In your own words, what's one BIG idea that will stick with you from this activity? In other words, what's an idea that you connected with or that made you think in a new way? Why was it impactful?

____

____

____

____

Essential Takeaway: Focusing on how you breathe is essential to managing your stress and anxiety. When you notice your stress levels rising, bring your attention to your breathing and make the necessary changes—breathe lightly, slowly, and deeply—to restore calm and emotional balance.

Section Three Reflection

Congrats! You've successfully completed another section of the workbook. Before you jump ahead, take a moment to bring it all together. I'll get you started:

- Your posture is important: stretch what is tight and strengthen what is weak so that you can sit up straight and breathe effortlessly and efficiently.
- Practice all three formal breathing postures and then decide which one works best for you and your mindful breathing practice.
- Shut your mouth and breathe through your nose!
- Breathe lightly, slowly, and deeply to restore inner calm.

____

____

Describe what was most impactful from section three.

____

____

How might this change what you do moving forward?

____

____

SECTION FOUR

Breathe Your Way to Self-Care

We've explored mindful breathing as a strategy to more skillfully exercise awareness and calm in the face of rising stress levels. But the truth is that in the long run, your mindful breathing practice alone won't transform stress into emotional strength. Your mindful breathing practice must be a part of a larger *self-care* practice. Remember that your breathing consistently tells you (via the breathing awareness exercises from activity 2) when your stress levels are rising. When this happens, it's a warning bell that you need to step up your mindful breathing and your self-care.

What is self-care? Self-care means just what it says: caring for yourself. Unfortunately, most of us struggle with properly caring for ourselves. We're too busy and distracted to stop and pay attention to and skillfully address the needs of our bodies and minds.

But when you fail to practice self-care, you ensure higher levels of stress and anxiety in your life. As I mentioned earlier in the workbook, the most skillful way to manage stress is to prevent it from getting out of control in the first place, and self-care is the art and practice of staying ahead of stress. After all, it takes more time, energy, and skill to slow down a stress and anxiety tailspin than it does to prevent yourself from spinning out in the first place.

14

make self-care deposits into your well-being account

Don't be fooled if this activity seems like a detour from mindful breathing—because it's not. As you already explored in section two, your breathing tells you when you're stressed out and overwhelmed. Sometimes mindful breathing alone is enough to downshift back into calm, but sometimes it's not. That's when our mindful breathing practice needs to work in tandem with a larger self-care practice—and that's what this activity is about.

Imagine that your well-being is a bank account. Now, with any bank account, you want to put in more money than you take out so that you can build your wealth instead of lose it (and risk going into debt). Similarly, with your well-being account, you want to put more self-care deposits into it than what you spend on your stress bills!

Self-Care Deposits

A self-care practice is a commitment to making regular self-care deposits in your wellbeing account. The more you make these deposits, the more the wealth of your wellbeing account grows. Here's a list of the main kinds of self-care deposits:

- quality sleep
- regular mindfulness and mindful breathing
- sufficient physical activity
- healthful eating
- meaningful social connection
- time spent in nature
- limited screen time

Are there any other kinds of self-care deposits that you enjoy and would add to this list? If so, write them here:

- __________________________________
- __________________________________
- __________________________________
- __________________________________
- __________________________________

Pick one kind of self-care deposit (other than mindful breathing) that you'd like to work on for one week. List that self-care deposit here: ______

Why did you choose this particular self-care deposit? For example, I picked healthful eating because of all the self-care deposits, I know that healthful eating is the one I struggle with the most, and not eating well elevates my stress levels over time. Okay, your turn.

____

____

____

____

What main factors have prevented you from making this kind of self-care deposit? For example, the factors that have stood in the way of my healthful eating are the fact that I exercise a lot, which makes me very, very hungry and more inclined to eat whatever I can get my hands on. I also don't have a structured eating plan that highlights what foods I'll buy and won't buy. As a result, I always have access to food I probably shouldn't be eating as much as I do (like banana chocolate chip ice cream! Ohhh boy. Deeeelicious). Alright enough about me. How about you?

____

____

____

____

Well done. You've identified a self-care deposit that you want to work on, why you want to work on it, and what obstacles you might encounter. Now, it's time to identify what you'll do differently over the course of the next week. For example, I'm going to sit down and write up a grocery list of all the things I should be eating and then list all the things I probably shouldn't buy at the store. Once I've done that, I'll create a general meal plan for the week so that I'm not aimlessly wandering through the kitchen at random times looking for something/anything to eat! What will you do?

____

____

____

____

Post-Week Reflection. How did your week go? What successes did you have with your self-care deposits? What struggles did you have? What opportunities for growth remain? For example, I ate way less ice cream than I usually do because I ate frozen berries with cashew milk instead. As the week went on, I struggled with sticking to the plan. My hunger and tastes led me astray a number of times, but luckily, I didn't veer too far off the path. My biggest opportunities for growth moving forward are getting better at planning and shopping. I know that after a couple more weeks of doing this, it'll all be second nature! Now, it's your turn.

Your self-care successes:

Your self-care struggles:

Your self-care opportunities:

Nicely done. But don't stop here. Continue to evaluate your self-care and what you can do to improve it. All of us have positive self-care habits that come naturally and others that require sustained effort and practice. Be easy on yourself and don't expect everything to change overnight. Real, enduring changes take time. So, be patient!

Stress Bills

The whole point of regularly making self-care deposits in your well-being account is to ensure that you have enough resources to pay your *stress bills*. Every aspect of your life requires these payments. Your ability to do algebra, learn French, memorize ancient Greek city-states, talk to friends, feel positive emotions, exercise, and peruse your social media account all create stress bills that are paid from your well-being account.

Making these payments is not a problem when you stay on schedule with your self-care deposits. But when you don't stay on schedule with your self-care deposits and your stress payments keep drawing from your well-being account, then you risk putting your well-being account into debt. And debt is worse than stress—because emotional debt creates *distress.* Distress is worse than stress because it's stress that feels unmanageable. And, when you get distressed, you get into all sorts of trouble because your ability to make good decisions is compromised.

Self-Care Loans

Once you're distressed, you're more likely to take out hasty *self-care loans* to temporarily get by. For example, when you don't make sleep a priority, you can't pay attention during your first period bio class, but you have to do well in the class to keep your GPA, so you're anxious—which is part of the reason why you're going to bed late and not sleeping well in the first place. So each morning you take out a small self-care loan: you go to the vending machine and purchase a highly caffeinated energy drink.

For a period or two, it seems as if this caffeinated windshield wiper fluid pays your stress bill for you, but all that it really does is delay your stress payment to a later time—which means that you'll have to deal with it again later and it will be more costly (after the caffeine crash).

You see, all loans have interest rates—which means that borrowed money (debt) grows and compounds the longer you don't pay it back. For example, when you continually don't sleep and take out daily caffeine loans to pay your stress bills, you start to pay your debt in more costly ways: your emotional stability waivers, your decision making weakens, and your focus blurs, to name a few.

Here's the truth: you can't get out of paying your stress bills. They never go away. You either practice self-care and have the resources up front to pay your stress bills or you borrow resources and pay in ways that are increasingly costly and self-destructive and that deplete your well-being. The only way to pay your stress bills on time is by making regular self-care deposits so that you always have enough resources in your well-being account to match your stress expenses.

Take a moment and imagine an ordinary day booked with stressful obligations like tests, essays, friend drama, extracurricular commitments, and so on. Now, imagine two versions of going through this imaginary day:

Version 1: You go through the day with skillful self-care practices, including sufficient sleep, good nutrition, plenty of physical activity, and healthy stress-management strategies (like mindful breathing).

Version 2: You go through the day with unskillful self-care practices, including insufficient sleep, poor nutrition, a lack of physical activity, and unhealthy stress-management strategies (like caffeine, drugs, or alcohol).

Which version of the day would likely be less stressful? Why?

____

____

____

____

Yes, the first version seems less stressful because you've deposited enough self-care resources into your well-being account to accommodate your daily stressors. Remember: not taking care of yourself is stressful!

How do you know when your well-being account is overdrawn (meaning you don't have enough in your account to cover your withdrawals, leaving you with a negative balance)? Well, the easiest way to know is based on how you feel. If your stress bucket is quickly heading to 10, then you're likely overdrawn.

Do you feel distressed on a daily or weekly basis? Does anxiety get in the way of feeling and living well? If so, explain your situation.

Does a lack of self-care contribute to your distress and anxiety? If so, how?

Do you regularly take out self-care loans to pay your stress bills? If so, what kind of self-care loans do you take out (e.g., caffeine, stress eating, alcohol, other substances)? And, more importantly, how do they impact your stress in the moment and over time?

Would the self-care deposit that you previously said you needed to work on help you stop using this self-care loan? If so, how? If not, then what's another self-care deposit that might help?

Okay. Thanks for doing this work. It's not always easy, but it's so important. Remember: when you take care of yourself, you take care of your stress.

BIG idea: In your own words, what's one BIG idea that will stick with your from this activity? In other words, what's an idea that you connected with or that made you think in a new way? Why was it impactful?

Essential Takeaway: The best way to manage stress is to stay ahead of it. Make regular self-care deposits into your well-being account. Many things in your life create stress bills, and if you've made regular self-care deposits into your well-being account, then you can make these stress payments without an issue and avoid the long-term stress that comes with taking out daily self-care loans.

Next, let's explore the most important self-care deposit that you can make in your wellbeing account: sleep.

15

exhale slowly to sleep better

Every aspect of your breathing, attention, stress, and emotional well-being reflects how well you sleep. It shouldn't surprise you, then, when I say that the most important self-care deposit you can make into your well-being account is sleep. The positive impact regular sleep deposits have on your well-being account are unmatched and unsurpassed. Regular sleep deposits alone are often enough to successfully pay off your stress bills. The truth is that even if everything in your self-care practice is on point, if your sleep is off, you're going to struggle with stress and emotion dysregulation.

Lucky for you, one of the best tools for getting a good night's sleep is learning how to calm yourself down before bed through mindful breathing. But before we get to that, let's briefly explore *why* sleep is so important for your ability to manage stress and protect your emotional well-being.

Why Sleep Matters

Why is sleep so important? Well, as sleep expert Matthew Walker says, the need for sleep is either nature's biggest mistake or nature's biggest secret for your stress management and your survival.[5] Adults need eight hours of sleep, and young adults likely need even more. But why would nature intend for you to be useless for one-third of your life?!

Long story short ... The need to sleep around eight hours a night is the cost of having such a remarkably high-powered brain. While you sleep, your brain cleans up the mess of information you've acquired throughout the day, organizes it, stores what is useful, discards the rest, and then does a deep clean so that your brain is nice and tidy when you wake up in the morning. This whole process, if done well, takes around eight hours.

One way to think about it is to consider your school building for a moment. Hundreds or thousands of people come into your school every day and use bathrooms, get floors muddy, fill garbage cans with trash, leave paper and debris everywhere, move furniture around, and destroy the cafeteria. But eventually everyone goes home, and when the building is empty, a special staff comes in and cleans the bathrooms and floors, takes out the trash, picks up the paper and debris, puts desks and chairs back in place, and cleans up the cafeteria. Then the next day, everyone comes back to a clean school building.

Sleep is the cleaning that happens in your brain after "everyone goes home." Now imagine if your school reduced the amount of time staff had to clean and take care of the building. Or imagine if they just didn't clean at all because no one went home. What would your school building look like if no one cleaned bathrooms and floors, emptied trash cans, picked up paper and debris, put desks and chairs back, and cleaned the cafeteria every night? Well, that's the condition of your brain when you don't sleep or don't sleep enough. Your brain becomes a mess. And when poor sleep continues night after night, year after year, it creates huge stress bills, dysregulates your breathing, and puts your well-being account into serious debt.

Let's not let that happen! In order to prevent the substantial loss of well-being created by a lack of sleep, let's look at your *sleep hygiene*—the habits and practices you've formed around sleep. If your sleep hygiene is on point, then you regularly wake up with enough physical and mental energy to meet the demands of your daily life (without caffeine or stimulants!).

Improve Your Sleep Hygiene

Good sleep hygiene is typically associated with these skillful habits:

- going to bed at the same time each night

- waking up at the same time each morning
- keeping your sleep environment quiet, dark, and cool
- staying off all screens and away from bright lights after 11p.m.
- getting sufficient outdoor physical activity during the day
- having a winding-down process before getting into bed

On the other hand, poor sleep hygiene is typically associated with these unskillful habits:

- regular phone/technology use past 11p.m.
- late night homework and studying
- caffeine consumption after dinner
- late night meals and snacks
- exercise late in the day (late sports practice or competition)
- insufficient physical activity during the day
- no winding-down process before getting into bed

Based on these sleep-hygiene descriptions, grade yourself on your sleep hygiene:

A = Outstanding. You sleep like an old dog on a cold winter night.

B = Good. You sleep well enough and often enough that you really don't have to think about sleep.

C = Needs some work. Every now and then, your sleep habits cause unnecessary stress and challenge your emotional well-being.

D = Struggling. Your sleep regularly causes stress and jeopardizes your emotional well-being.

F = Failing. Poor sleep is ruining your life. You need something to change fast.

My sleep-hygiene grade: ______

Why did you give yourself this grade?

____

____

____

____

What sleep-hygiene habit is most detrimental to your ability to sleep? What can you do to change this?

____

____

____

____

Bravo! Strong effort. I hope you have a better handle on why sleep is such a big deal. Don't wait to make the changes you need to make in order to sleep better. Start tonight!

Mindfully Breathe to Wind Down

Countless students have voiced to me that they struggle to fall asleep. When it's time to go to bed, their brains feel like a tornado spinning out of control. And because they struggle to fall asleep, they use their phones to distract themselves until they eventually fall asleep. The problem with this is that when you view any bright light at night (after 11p.m.), especially the blue light emitted from your phone or computer, it activates circuits in your brain that impact your ability to sleep well. Additionally, these same circuits impact your memory, learning, and emotions.[6] Ironically, when you use your phone or computer as a means to wind your brain down, you're actually ramping it up—which disrupts how long you're going to sleep and how deeply. In short, winding down with phones and computers is a self-care loan that will bankrupt your well-being account!

Here's a little secret I share with my students: instead of using phones or computers to wind down, practice mindful breathing before bed and achieve better results without the negative side effects. With a little discipline and practice, you will sleep better and find your well-being account full when you wake in the morning.

Here's what you need to do to get started:

Step 1: Determine a specific bedtime, ideally before 11p.m. After 11p.m., you're starting to cut into the time of night your brain is primed for different sleep operations.

Step 2: Designate a specific place that is quiet and clutter free, where you can do your mindful breathing about fifteen minutes before your designated bedtime.

Step 3: Get into comfy clothing.

Step 4: Dim the lights if you can. You don't want bright light and you don't want it totally dark to start.

Step 5: Find a comfortable breathing position (refer back to activity 11 in section three) and spot in the room. I often recommend sitting up first and then allowing yourself to transition to lying down as you get tired.

Okay, good. Now the breathing part...

Step 1: Take at least two to three minutes to just consciously breathe through your nose. You don't need to change your breathing yet. Just allow your attention to slowly settle on your breathing as it is. As you do this, nonjudgmentally notice the different qualities of your breathing and your overall state. If any strong thoughts or feelings are present, simply notice them and then feel your breathing and your body as a whole. Feel all the places of your body, especially the areas that ordinarily escape attention, like the tops of your feet and hands. If you want, you can place a hand on your chest and a hand on your lower abdomen to provide a more distinct sense of your breathing. Some people also find this comforting.

As you anchor attention on your breathing, gently expand your attention and nonjudgmentally notice any areas of tension in your body and simply continue to consciously breathe. The whole point here is to allow your mind and body a transitional phase between the activity of the day and going to sleep.

Step 2: Now that you've settled into your breathing and a sense of your body as a whole, it's time to consciously regulate your breathing. For a few minutes, consciously slow your breathing down (still breathing through the nose). Ideally, you'd breathe in for around six seconds and then breathe out for around six seconds. If you can't breathe in for six seconds and out for six seconds, then try five seconds. If you can't do five seconds, then try four seconds. You get the idea: just breathe slowly and equally in and out.

Step 3: Continue to breathe slowly, but now shift your focus to your exhales. You're going to slow your exhales down even more than your inhales. Ideally, you'd breathe in for six seconds and out for twelve seconds (it's okay, not everyone can do this right away). All you need to remember is that for however many seconds you breathe in, just double that number on your exhalation. Here's a quick chart:

Winding-Down Breathing Chart

Inhale	Pause	Exhale
1 Second	1 Second	2 Seconds
2 Seconds	1 Second	4 Seconds
3 Seconds	1 Second	6 Seconds
4 Seconds	1 Second	8 Seconds
5 Seconds	1 Second	10 Seconds
6 Seconds	1 Second	12 Seconds

Continue to breathe this way for as long as you'd like. Within five minutes you should definitely feel your body and mind relax. Once you transition from calm to sleepy, just turn your light off, get into bed, and continue breathing this way until you fall asleep.

Now, if you want an even more potent variation of this exercise, lengthen the pause after you inhale. Extending that pause to at least the amount of seconds you inhale is a good place to start. Eventually, you'd want to work up to a 1:4:2 breathing ratio. Here's the chart.

Inhale	Pause	Exhale
1 Second	4 Seconds	2 Seconds
2 Seconds	8 Seconds	4 Seconds
3 Seconds	12 Seconds	6 Seconds
4 Seconds	16 Seconds	8 Seconds
5 Seconds	20 Seconds	10 Seconds
6 Seconds	24 Seconds	12 Seconds

Don't force the pause. If you're strained in any way, you're pausing too long and the exercise will not calm you down. Play around with these techniques and see what works. As a rule of thumb, the slower you breathe and the longer you exhale, the calmer you'll feel. This is a skill, which means it takes time to master it. Be patient. Gradually build up.

If all of these charts and numbers seem confusing or overwhelming, then just remember: *breathe slowly through your nose.* Just doing this alone will significantly help.

Commit to this mindful breathing practice each night for one week. At the end of the week, give yourself a new grade on your sleep hygiene. Refer to the aforementioned qualities of good sleep. Here's your sleep hygiene rubric again:

A = Outstanding. You sleep like an old dog on a cold winter night.

B = Good. You sleep well enough and often enough that you really don't have to think about sleep.

C = Needs some work. Every now and then, your sleep habits cause unnecessary stress and challenge your emotional well-being.

D = Struggling. Your sleep regularly causes stress and jeopardizes your emotional well-being.

F = Failing. Poor sleep is ruining your life. You need something to change fast.

My new sleep hygiene grade: ______

Did you practice mindful breathing each night? ______

Did you follow the recommended steps for practicing? ______

Why did you give yourself this grade?

____

____

____

____

Did your sleep-hygiene grade change for better or worse? What do you attribute this to?

____

____

____

____

What impact did mindful breathing have on your sleep hygiene?

Nicely done. From my experience, if you commit yourself to mindful breathing, it will improve your ability to downshift, especially before bed. It might take some time to get your own pre-bedtime routine down, so be patient and persistent. Good habits need time to take root.

BIG Idea: In your own words, what's one BIG idea that will stick with you from this activity? In other words, what's an idea that you connected with or that made you think in a new way? Why was it impactful?

Essential Takeaway: Quality sleep is the most important self-care deposit that you can make in your well-being account. A consistent lack of sleep can cause stress and disrupt your emotional well-being. To ensure that you get the most out of your sleep, you must practice good sleep-hygiene habits like mindful breathing.

169

Practice mindful breathing before bedtime as a way of winding down and preparing yourself to get the most out of your sleep.

16

write, live, and breathe your life philosophy

One of the least talked about and most underutilized self-care strategies is developing your own life philosophy. What's a life philosophy? Most simply stated, it's what you believe to be most valuable, meaningful, and true about life in general and yourself specifically.

Think of your life philosophy this way ... In the same way that ancient travelers followed the North Star to guide their travels, your life philosophy is your North Star guiding you on your life's journey. Without a guiding star (life philosophy), you'll easily wander and get lost—and being lost is stressful and definitely not how you want to travel through life!

Write Your Life Philosophy

When I initially ask students if they have a life philosophy, they often immediately say that they do. But when I ask them what it is, they look at me with a blank stare. The truth is that most of us assume that we know our life philosophy, but when we're asked on the spot to clearly and succinctly state what it is, we quickly realize that we have no idea what to say! But here's the thing: you have to clearly know your life philosophy before you can live it. So, let's get you writing...

Finish these prompts.

(Quick note: For the "I" prompts, feel free to switch the "I" to "people." Sometimes it's less intimidating to finish the prompts in the third person).

I believe that I should think...

____

____

I believe that I should feel...

____

____

I believe that I should say...

____

____

I believe that I should do...

____

____

I believe that I should be...

____

____

I believe that life is...

____

____

I believe that the most valuable things (objects, feelings, people, places, anything) in life are...

I believe that success is...

I believe that failure is...

My life's purpose is to...

No matter what, I'll never forget that...

Whoa. That was some heavy mental lifting. Pat yourself on the back and give yourself a well-deserved break.

[Intermission] Your favorite music playing in the background...

Okay, we're back. Now take a step back, look at what you wrote, and see if you can find an underlying theme or themes running through your responses. For example, circle words that you repeat—words like "kindness," "patience," "strength," "calm," and so on.

List those themes here:

____

____

____

____

____

Now ask yourself where you learned those themes. For example, where and from whom did you learn the importance of kindness?

Theme	Where or from whom did you learn it?

Alright, I think you're ready. I'd like you to write a paragraph stating your life philosophy. I would provide an example, but I've found that for students who are reluctant, they end up imitating the example, which prevents them from truly *owning* what they're writing. And ownership is the foundation of having your own philosophy—because it's based on your unique experiences, values, and beliefs and no one else's.

Use the responses that you've already completed to get you going.

This doesn't have to be perfect on the first try. In fact, it will never be perfect because you're always in the process of becoming who you are—and that means your philosophy will always be evolving. Think of this as a snapshot of what you believe to be most valuable, meaningful, and true right now in your life.

Okay, okay. I'm done talking. Ready, set, go...

____

____

____

____

____

____

____

____

____

____

Whew. I'm proud of you. Seriously. More importantly, you should be proud of yourself. Not many people take the time to mindfully reflect on and write down their own life philosophy. As I say to my students, this should be the first of many times you do this exercise.

But you're not quite off the hook yet. Yup, there's more to do. When you're ready, take your life philosophy statement and reduce it to three words or less. I'll provide one example to help get you started. This is a student's three-word statement from this past school year: "Be. Here. Now."

Here's a doodle box to play around with word combinations:

-
-
-
-
-
-
-
-
-
-

Now it's time to commit. Again, nothing is final. You can change and rewrite this tomorrow if you're compelled to do so.

Write your three-word or less personal life philosophy statement right here and add your name below:

____

(______'s Life Philosophy Statement)

Take this statement, write it on any piece of paper, and put it somewhere you're going to see it every day. For example, my students have put it on their nightstands, on their bedroom ceilings, in their wallets, on their bathroom mirrors, on their locker doors, and on their car dashboards.

The idea is that you now have a clear reminder, a North Star, to hang in as many places as you need to remind you of the life path you want to be on, the one that leads you to your deepest values, beliefs, and aspirations.

Now it's time to live your life philosophy!

Live Your Life Philosophy

It's important to recognize that distraction jeopardizes your ability to live your life philosophy in real time. When you're distracted, you forget about your North Star—your life philosophy—and you wander away from the core beliefs and values central to living your best life.

How do you combat distraction? How do you keep your eyes on your personal philosophy? You do this by identifying the *people*, *activities*, and *places* that connect you to your life philosophy, that make your philosophy come to life, and then you build your schedule around these things. As the old adage exclaims, "Don't prioritize your schedule; schedule your priorities!"

Here we go...

People to Connect With

List each person who connects you to your life philosophy and then explain how they connect you to your philosophy (for example, my grandfather because he always had a smile on his face and found a way to connect with anyone he met. He always looked for the good in people). And last, designate how often you need to connect with this person: Multiple times a day? Once a day? Once a week?

Person: ____

This person connects me to my life philosophy because they...

____

____

I need to connect with this person...

____

Person: ____

This person connects me to my life philosophy because they...

____

____

I need to connect with this person...

____

Person: ____

This person connects me to my life philosophy because they...

I need to connect with this person...

Person: _____
This person connects me to my life philosophy because they...

I need to connect with this person...

Person: _____
This person connects me to my life philosophy because they...

I need to connect with this person...

Places to Connect With

List each place that connects you to your life philosophy and then explain how it connects you to your philosophy (for example, I need to walk at the forest preserve because it opens a space inside of me where I can process everything that's going on in my life). And last, designate how often you need to connect with this place: Multiple times a day? Once a day? Once a week?

Place: _____

This place connects me to my life philosophy because it...

____

____

I need to connect with this place...

____

Place: _____

This place connects me to my life philosophy because it...

____

____

I need to connect with this place...

____

Place: _____

This place connects me to my life philosophy because it...

____

____

I need to connect with this place...

____

Place: _____

This place connects me to my life philosophy because it...

I need to connect with this place...

Place: _____

This place connects me to my life philosophy because it...

I need to connect with this place...

Activities to Connect With

List each activity that connects you to your life philosophy and then explain how it connects you to your philosophy (for example, I love to draw because it allows me to tap into my creativity and see things in a new light). And last, designate how often you need to do this activity in order to connect with your life philosophy: Multiple times a day? Once a day? Once a week?

Activity: _____

This activity connects me to my life philosophy because it...

I need to do this activity...

Activity: _____

This activity connects me to my life philosophy because it...

I need to do this activity...

Activity: _____

This activity connects me to my life philosophy because it...

I need to do this activity...

Activity: _____

This activity connects me to my life philosophy because it...

I need to do this activity...

Activity: _____

This activity connects me to my life philosophy because it...

I need to do this activity...

You have a limited amount of time on this planet, so you need to make decisions about how you will spend your time. From my experience working with young adults, I've seen a recurring pattern: issues with *stress management* are often issues with *time management*—which are really issues with *priority management.* And when you don't manage your priorities—like scheduling time to connect with the people, activities, and places that make your life philosophy come alive—you'll easily get distracted, forget what you value, and burn yourself out.

Begin and End Each Day Breathing Your Life Philosophy

At the heart of every life philosophy is an increased awareness of and attentiveness to what is most important about our lives. This awareness and attentiveness to what is most important is also at the heart of mindful breathing. Beyond managing stress and increasing emotional well-being and freedom, mindful breathing is really about connecting with what is most true and enduring about ourselves and our lives.

I often say to students that mindful breathing helps us see that what is most personal is also most universal. What I mean by this is that when you use your breathing to connect with the core of who you are—your struggles, hopes, and values—you start to see that your individual life is playing out a timeless human drama. Everyone who has ever lived has had to find a way to deal with the conflicts and stressors that are inherently a part of life. Mindful breathing brings you right to the center of our shared human experience and allows you to navigate it with more intelligence and care—so that, ultimately, you can share your inner calm, perspective, and insight with others.

As our time together comes to an end, your head might be spinning from all the information I've shared in this workbook. There's no need to worry though—I'll leave you with a simple recommendation and exercise: begin and end each day mindfully breathing your life philosophy.

To begin this exercise, follow the basic protocols already established: find somewhere clean and quiet, wear comfy clothes, have a straight spine, breathe through your nose, and just start by watching your breath for a few minutes. Once you've done all of this, try the following:

Step 1: As you breathe in, imagine breathing in your three-word life philosophy statement. I don't just mean the words—I mean what the words mean to you, the life that they give you. As you breathe in, imagine breathing in the love you have for the people, activities, and places that you listed. Imagine breathing in all of that positive, life-giving energy with every breath.

Step 2: When you exhale, imagine breathing out everything else that competes for your attention: all the distractions, frustrations, expectations, and disappointments. Just let all of it go with every breath. And by exhaling all of that clutter, you open a huge space inside yourself to be filled with the next life-giving breath.

Practice this morning and night and mindfully breathe your philosophy into reality.

BIG Idea: In your own words, what's one BIG idea that will stick with you from this activity? In other words, what's an idea that you connected with or that made you think in a new way? Why was it impactful?

____

____

____

____

Essential Takeaway: As you deepen your self-care, don't underestimate or forget the significance of clearly knowing and stating your life philosophy. Once you've penned it, breathe it and let your highest aspiration and values fill your being with every breath. And let go of the rest.

parting thought: make the most of your 30,000 pebbles

I want you to imagine a jar with 30,000 pebbles in it. Why 30,000? Because the average person in the modern world lives about 30,000 days, but of course, this is an average, not a guarantee. So, imagine that each pebble is a day. This means that every morning when you wake up and hit "snooze," you're making an important decision about how you value your time.

That's right. There are no do-overs or put-backs. Every day is a pebble pulled out of the jar of your life, and you can mindlessly discard it or you can begin to more seriously consider: what can I do with this pebble, this day, that honors its true value? Because time is a nonrenewable resource, and each pebble, each day, slips through your hands, never to be retrieved again.

It's my sincerest hope that you've learned something in this workbook that will help you more fully honor the "pebble," this gift of a day, that you hold in your hand. Thank you for being brave and dedicated. Remember, becoming your own person is a process, not a destination. Be kind and patient with yourself (and others, too). Breathe mindfully and enjoy yourself along the way!

All the best,

Mr. D

acknowledgements

First and foremost, I want to thank Tracy Heilers and Gina Biegel, two amazing women and friends championing mindfulness for students, educators, schools, and communities. This book would not have happened without them.

I am grateful for and indebted to the work and teaching of Rob Wilson and Patrick McKeown, two exceptional breathing instructors who help people all over the world reclaim their physical and emotional health through conscious breathing. This workbook attests to their influence.

Thank you to everyone on the New Harbinger team who supported this project. Thanks to Jennifer Holder and Rona Bernstein, my amazing editors. A special thanks to Jess O'Brien, my invaluable acquisitions editor, who got this book off the ground and guided me through this journey from day one.

Everything in this book is inspired by and deeply rooted in my daily work with the students at Lake Forest High School and for that I am indebted to them. Special thanks to my former students JR Reimer, Mari Danneker, and Emily Mangione, who provided invaluable feedback on drafts and to Tara Brunner for designing the illustrations throughout this workbook.

Last, I want to thank my wife, Katie, my stepson, Max, and our two golden retrievers,

Winny and Moose. They get to deal with the not-so-great version of me that emerges when deadlines approach. I love you and am so lucky to have a home where I am loved ... even when I don't deserve it!

endnotes

[1] Yackle, K., Schwarz, L., Kam, K., Sorokin, J., Huguenard, J., Feldman, J., et al. 2017. "Breathing control center neurons that promote arousal in mice." *Science* 355: 1411-1415.

[2] Crangle, E.F. 1994. *The Origin and Development of Early Indian Contemplative Practices.* Weisbaden, Germany: Otto Harrassowitz Verlag.

[3] Herrero, J.L., S. Khuvis, E. Yeagle, M. Cerf, and A.D. Mehta. 2018. "Breathing Above the Brain Stem: Volitional Control and Attentional Modulation in Humans." *Journal of Neurophysiology* 119(1): 145–159. https://doi.org/10.1152/jn.00551.2017

[4] The interpretation of these carbon dioxide tolerance scores is based on McKeown, P. 2015. *The Oxygen Advantage: The Simple, Scientifically Proven Breathing Techniques for a Healthier, Slimmer, Faster, and Fitter You.* New York, NY: HarperCollins.

[5] Walker, M. 2018. *Why We Sleep.* London, UK: Penguin Books.

[6] LeGates, T.A., D.C. Fernandez, and S. Hattar. 2014. "Light as a Central Modulator of Circadian Rhythms, Sleep

and Affect." *Nature Reviews Neuroscience* 15: 443–454 https://www.nature.com/articles/nrn3743

Matthew D. Dewar, EdD, is a professional educator and author working at the intersection of mindfulness, self-regulation, and emotional resilience. For nearly two decades, Matt has served as an educator and well-being coordinator at Lake Forest High School in Illinois. Trained in curriculum and social-emotional learning, Matt earned his doctorate from the National College of Education. He is also former president of the Coalition of Schools Educating Mindfully (COSEM), serves on its board, and consults with school districts nationally on implementing mindfulness and emotional well-being programming.

Foreword writer **Gina M. Biegel, MA, LMFT,** is a psychotherapist, researcher, speaker, and author in the San Francisco Bay Area who specializes in mindfulness-based work with adolescents. An expert and pioneer in bringing mindfulness-based approaches to youth, she is author of *The Stress Reduction Workbook for Teens* and the *Be Mindful Card Deck for Teens*. For more information, visit her website at www.stressedteens.com.

Did you know there are free tools you can download for this book?

Free tools are things like **worksheets, guided meditation exercises**, and **more** that will help you get the most out of your book.

You can download free tools for this book—whether you bought or borrowed it, in any format, from any source—from the **New Harbinger** website. All you need is a NewHarbinger.com account. Just use the URL provided in this book to view the free tools that are available for it. Then, click on the "download" button for the free tool you want, and follow the prompts that appear to log in to your NewHarbinger.com account and download the material.

You can also save the free tools for this book to your **Free Tools Library** so you can access them again anytime, just by logging in to your account! Just look for this button on the book's free tools page:

+ save this to my free tools library

If you need help accessing or downloading free tools, visit **newharbinger.com/faq** or contact us at customerservice@newharbinger.com.

Back Cover Material

use mindful breathing to **transform stress** into **strength**

Are you stressed out or overwhelmed? Do you ever feel like there's just *too much* to do, and not enough time to do it? If so, you're far from alone. Many teens feel stress due to academic pressure, high expectations from family and friends, social media overload, and an increasingly uncertain future. The good news is there's a powerful tool you can use to manage stress-filled moments, life changes big and small, and those daily setbacks that keep you from being your best. It's called *mindful breathing*—and this workbook will teach you all about it.

In this fun and engaging guide, you'll learn breathing skills and simple self-care strategies to help you stay grounded, find calm, and get out of bad moods quickly. By developing your own personalized tool kit for managing stress, you will feel stronger and more in control—even when faced with difficult situations beyond your control.

THIS WORKBOOK WILL HELP YOU:

* Relax your body in times of stress
* Cultivate mindful attention
* Balance intense emotions
* Reach your goals

"A practical guide to mindfully balance your breath, body, emotions, and stress."
—CHRISTOPHER WILLARD, PsyD, author of *Growing Up Mindful;* faculty at Harvard Medical School

MATTHEW D. DEWAR, EDD, is a professional educator and author working at the intersection of mindfulness, self-regulation, and emotional resilience. Matt is an educator and well-being coordinator at Lake Forest High School in Illinois, and consults with school districts nationally on implementing mindfulness and emotional well-being programming.

www.ingramcontent.com/pod-product-compliance
Lightning Source LLC
LaVergne TN
LVHW030913080826
845145LV00011B/2880